TIMBER PRESS
POCKET GUIDE TO
Ornamental
Grasses

TIMBER PRESS
POCKET GUIDE TO
Ornamental Grasses

TEXT AND PHOTOGRAPHY BY
RICK DARKE

TIMBER PRESS
Portland ◆ Cambridge

Frontispiece: The autumn glow of sunlit wild-oats, *Chasmanthium latifolium*, is intensified by a background of shadow and the blue hue of native asters in the author's garden (Pennsylvania) in mid-October.

Text and photographs copyright © 2004 by Rick Darke

Published in 2004 by

Timber Press, Inc.   Timber Press
The Haseltine Building   2 Station Road
133 S.W. Second Avenue, Suite 450   Swavesey
Portland, Oregon 97204-3527, U.S.A.   Cambridge CB4 5QJ, U.K.

www.timberpress.com

Printed through Colorcraft Ltd., Hong Kong

Library of Congress Cataloging-in-Publication Data

Darke, Rick.
    Pocket guide to ornamental grasses / text and photography by
Rick Darke.
        p. cm. —   (Timber Press pocket guides)
    Includes bibliographical references (p.   ).
    ISBN 0-88192-653-1 (flexibind)
    1. Ornamental grasses--Handbooks, manuals, etc. I. Title. II. Series.

    SB431.7.D372 2004
    635.9'349--dc22
                                                    2004000000

A catalog record for this book is also available from the British Library.

Acknowledgments

Thanks again to all those people and places mentioned in *The Color Encyclopedia of Ornamental Grasses*, on which this pocket guide is based, and to the ever-growing international community of friends and professional acquaintances who so generously share their knowledge and appreciation of grasses in the global landscape.

All black-and-white illustrations, unless individually credited otherwise, were adapted from USDA Miscellaneous Publication No. 200, the classic 1951 revision of the *Manual of the Grasses of the United States* by A. S. Hitchcock and Agnes Chase. All color photographs are my own; most were taken with a Nikon FM2 film camera using Kodachrome ASA 64 film, and several images were produced with a Sony F717 digital camera.

About This Book

The entries in this pocket guide are arranged in alphabetical order by scientific name. If a genus or species name appears to be missing from this alphabetical listing, it may be because the name has been changed by taxonomists. To find the current name, look up the "missing" name in the Index. Cultivar names are enclosed by single quotation marks. Synonyms for cultivars, if any, follow the current name and are enclosed in parentheses. Zone numbers refer to the lowest USDA cold-hardiness zone in which the grasses will survive.

CONTENTS

Opposite: *Carex oshimensis* 'Evergold' in late July in British Columbia.

PREFACE

In the laying out of lawns and artistic gardens, a few of the many beautiful hardy grasses should not be overlooked. Their stateliness, tropic luxuriance, and soft colors harmoniously punctuate the prevailing green, while their graceful, sinuous yielding to every wind gives animation to gardened landscapes too apt to look "fixed."

Spring 1909 Catalog, The Storrs and
Harrison Company, Painesville, Ohio

Looking back at ornamental grasses and their role in gardens over the past century, it is easy to see that much has changed. Whereas gardeners at the turn of the twentieth century had perhaps a dozen perennial grasses to choose from, today's gardeners have hundreds. Ornamental grasses now embody a huge array of textures, forms, sizes, colors, flowering times, and cultural adaptations. This exhilarating increase in diversity has resulted from the efforts of botanists, breeders, and nurseries in nearly all parts of the world and seems certain to continue. The unprecedented popularity grasses now enjoy can be attributed partly to this development; however, there are other factors fueling the current enthusiasm that are sure to influence the place grasses will hold in tomorrow's gardens.

In an age of increasingly rapid change, we are doing more than expanding the plant palette—we are redefining the garden. Landscape gardening, that unique confluence of art and science, is searching for a model that will provide an opportunity for creative expression and a reverent link to the larger ecology. Gardens must be at once inspiring and conserving, high-spirited and low maintenance. They must reflect and sustain the rhythms of our lives, our homes, and our shared places, and they must speak to us eloquently of the sun and seasons. Delightfully, there are grasses suited to all these ideals.

Drawn from the experience and creativity of great gardens and gardeners around the world, this book is intended for gardeners in a wide range of situations and climates, providing a uniquely thorough yet conveniently portable guide to the selection and identification of the modern palette of ornamental grasses.

Opposite: Standing tall above still-blooming frost asters, *Andropogon gerardii* contributes rich copper tones to a prairie restoration in Lake Bluff, Illinois, in late October.

INTRODUCTION

Gardeners usually speak of *ornamental grasses* in the broad sense, including not only the true grasses, but also related families of grasslike plants, such as sedges and rushes. Following this tradition, this pocket guide includes the perennial grasses (grass family), sedges (sedge family), rushes (rush family), restios (restio family), and cat-tails (cat-tail family).

Ornamental grasses thrive in a range of climatic and cultural conditions. Properly selected and used, grasses can contribute more beauty and interest with less maintenance than almost any other group of garden perennials. This introduction offers general approaches, techniques, and recommendations to help gardeners get the most from the grasses they grow. Additional comments and recommendations specific to individual grasses appear in the plant descriptions.

Growth Habits: Runners and Clumpers

Though technically all grasses increase in width or spread to some degree by lateral shoots, for garden purposes it is common and practical to group grasses as either runners or clumpers.

Running grasses spread rather rapidly by rhizomes, in which case they may also be called *rhizomatous* grasses, or by stolons, in which case they may be called *stoloniferous*. Most running ornamental grasses are rhizomatous. Stoloniferous growth is more common among turf grasses and weedy species, such as crab grasses, *Digitaria* species.

When used appropriately, running grasses can minimize maintenance. Their ability to knit together and cover large areas often makes them the best choice for groundcover use and soil stabilization. Running grasses are able to fill in gaps that may appear in a planting due to physical damage or disease, and many are so dense and

strong in their growth that they keep weeds from establishing. In extremely difficult sites, such as urban traffic islands, running grasses are often the most practical choice. Some running types, such as gold-edged cordgrass, *Spartina pectinata* 'Aureomarginata', are tolerant of moist or wet soils and can be ideal for holding streambanks and margins of ponds or storm water retention basins.

When planted in the wrong situation, however, running grasses can cause serious problems in the garden. They can completely overpower less vigorous neighbors and turn once-diverse borders into monocultures. Before planting a strongly running grass, carefully consider whether adjacent plantings and hardscapes are sturdy enough to contain its spread and whether someone will have the time and energy for removing its advances into unwanted areas.

The vigor of running species varies radically with climate and cultural conditions in the garden. For example, a warm-season spreader like giant reed, *Arundo donax*, may be unmanageable in a small garden in sunny Georgia, whereas the short, cool season of a Connecticut garden may slow it to the point that it behaves more like a clumping grass.

Clumping grasses essentially remain in place. They may slowly increase in girth, but new shoots will not appear at distances from the clump. Grasses that produce tight clumps are also referred to as tufted, caespitose, or bunchgrasses. Though clump-forming grasses may take many years to reach mature size, the ultimate space they consume in the garden is more predictable, and for this reason they are often easier to design with than running types. Because they are not able to fill in large gaps between individual plants, however, they can sometimes require more long-term maintenance than running grasses when

Opposite: *Miscanthus sinensis* is embraced by the winter berries of *Ilex verticillata* along a Delaware sidewalk at the end of December.

used as groundcovers, as happens with ground-cover plantings of blue fescue, *Festuca glauca*.

A few grasses do not fit neatly into either the running or clumping categories. The growth habit of Hakone grass, *Hakonechloa macra*, has been variously described as caespitose and spreading. This grass increases by rhizomes and is capable of continuous spread if cultural conditions are ideal, yet its rate of increase is often so modest that, for most gardeners, it is a clump-former in the practical sense. Switchgrass, *Panicum virgatum*, is also somewhere between strictly clump-forming and running. Its rhizomes occasionally stray noticeably from the clump, yet for most intents and purposes it is a clumping grass.

The running or clumping nature of grasses can vary between species belonging to the same genus. For example, *Miscanthus* and *Pennisetum* each include strictly clumping species as well as aggressively running species.

Growing Seasons: Warm and Cool

Although grasses from tropical climates are often capable of continuous, year-round growth, most ornamental grasses evolved in temperate or Mediterranean climates. There they developed cycles of growth in response to different seasonal opportunities and limitations. In cold-temperate climates, for example, winter cold may be the ultimate limitation to growth, whereas in Mediterranean climates, summer drought often checks growth.

In a broad sense grasses can be grouped as cool-season growers and warm-season growers. Temperature governs the periods of active growth as do light intensity and available moisture, factors that can be modified by gardening techniques. A basic familiarity with plant responses to cultural and climatic patterns will help in making informed decisions about selecting grasses for a particular climate as well as choosing optimum times for planting and dividing ornamental grasses.

Cool-season grasses grow well in temperatures from near freezing up to approximately 75°F (24°C). In a cold-temperate climate this means

they often have two periods of growth. Typically they begin growth in late winter, develop significant foliage by early spring, and produce flowers anytime from late winter to early summer. This growth period coincides with a combination of moisture, warmth, and sunlight ideally suited to the metabolism and photosynthetic processes of this type of grass. As the summer progresses, temperature and sunlight intensity increase, often accompanied by a decrease in rainfall. These conditions are stressful to the metabolism of cool-season grasses. Unable to take advantage of the additional sunlight because of the excessive heat and lack of moisture, the plants capture less net energy and usually go partly or fully dormant. Cool-season grasses resume growth when sunlight wanes, temperatures drop, and rainfall increases at summer's end. They continue growing until extreme winter temperatures force a complete cessation of growth.

Cool-season grasses may be divided or transplanted from late winter into early spring and again from late summer to midautumn. They should not be moved or divided as they approach or are in their summer dormant state, however partial it may be. Planting these grasses in areas partially shaded in summer can relieve the stress of summer to some extent. Supplemental watering during summer droughts can also be helpful and may keep some species from going dormant. In cooler climates, many cool-season grasses are evergreen or semi-evergreen.

Not all cool-season grasses are alike in their physiological behavior. Striped tuber oat grass, *Arrhenatherum elatius* subsp. *bulbosum* 'Variegatum', is an example of an extreme cool-season grower. It begins growth with the first warm days of winter or remains evergreen though mild winters. It blooms in spring and then goes completely dormant in the middle of a hot, dry summer. An effective design strategy is to situate other plants with summer interest to mask the dormant grass until it puts on a flush of fresh new growth as autumn begins.

Feather reed grass, *Calamagrostis* ×*acutiflora* 'Karl Foerster', is also a cool-season grower, but is

Amid a rich mix of green companions, the chartreuse foliage of *Carex elata* 'Aurea' (center) contrasts with the subtly striped leaves of *Hakonechloa macra* 'Albovariegata' in mid-May in the author's Pennsylvania garden.

much more tolerant of summer conditions. Although its growth will slow, it remains green and reasonably attractive in all but the worst summers. Other examples of cool-season grasses are blue oat grass, *Helictotrichon sempervirens*; most fescues, *Festuca* species; melic grasses, *Melica* species; and most *Stipa* and *Achnatherum* species.

Warm-season grasses like it hot. Although their metabolisms are less efficient than cool-season growers at lower temperatures, they are superbly adapted to temperatures of 80–95°F (24–27°C). Warm-season growers typically break winter dormancy late in spring and are very slow growing until summer arrives. They revel in the intense summer sun, growing steadily larger and gathering energy until they flower at summer's end. Their processes shut down with the onset of cold weather, and they remain dormant through winter. During this shutdown, many warm-season grasses take on beautiful autumn colors.

Warm-season grasses are best divided or transplanted when they are in active growth but long before they begin blooming. Late spring into early summer is an ideal time. It can be risky to divide or transplant them in fall because much of the plants' stored energy often has just been spent on flower and seed production. In cold climates, fall divisions and transplants will make very little new growth before winter dormancy begins, and the plants will be forced to endure the stresses of freezing temperatures, and often excessive moisture, with depleted energy reserves. Fall transplanting works well only in mild climates. It is usually least successful in climates approaching the winter cold hardiness of the grasses in question.

The various *Miscanthus* species; pampas grasses, *Cortaderia* species; giant reed, *Arundo donax*; and the fountain grasses, *Pennisetum* species, are examples of warm-season growers, as are many North American natives, such as little

Illuminated by summer sunlight, the graceful, arching foliage of *Miscanthus sinensis* 'Morning Light' frames the entrance to a path in Washington State.

bluestem, *Schizachyrium scoparium*; big bluestem, *Andropogon gerardii*; switchgrass, *Panicum virgatum*; and Indian grass, *Sorghastrum nutans*.

Sun and Shade

Generally, true grasses thrive in sunny situations, and sedges and wood-rushes tend to prefer shade; however, there are many exceptions. Individual preferences of various species and cultivars are included in plant descriptions.

Most sun-loving grasses perform adequately if provided three to five hours of direct sun each day. They are stronger and more upright in more sun and weaker and somewhat lax in less. Large sun-loving grasses, such as *Miscanthus*, are more prone to falling over in shaded situations if soils are highly fertile.

Other than flowers, the peak attraction of many grasses is their autumn foliage color, which is usually most pronounced in high sun situa-

tions. Although a few variegated grasses, such as Hakone grass, *Hakonechloa*, require partial shade, bright sunlight brings out the best in most variegated grasses, sedges, and rushes.

Remember that the intensity of "full sun" differs dramatically in various parts of the world. Full sun in Cornwall, England, is more like part shade in southern California. Full sun at high mountain elevations, which are often cloaked in clouds, may also equate to shade at valley bottoms.

Soils

One of the reasons grasses are so popular is that they often thrive in what gardeners are wont to refer to as "bad" soils. While most grasses appreciate a well-drained, reasonably fertile loam, the many adaptable sorts, including *Miscanthus*, are undaunted by either poorly drained heavy clays or dry infertile sands. As a group, grasses are also largely indifferent to normal variations in acidity and alkalinity, and many, especially the coastal species, are somewhat salt tolerant.

Soil differences, however, can make a real difference in the performance of certain ornamental grasses. For example, some grasses, including the popular cultivars of blue fescue, *Festuca glauca*, require sharp drainage if they are to survive cold wet winters in good condition. Running grasses, such as blue lyme grass, *Leymus arenarius*, may be manageable in dense clays but too aggressive in rich friable loam. Well-aerated soils high in organic matter are necessary for best growth on a few of the woodland sedges, including Fraser's sedge, *Cymophyllus fraserianus*.

Fertilization

I have gardened for more than two decades without having ever directly fertilized a grass. Except when grown on sterile sands, ornamental grasses generally do not benefit from supplemental fertilization: typical garden soils offer adequate or sometimes more than adequate fertility. Adding concentrated chemical fertilizers to typical soils can actually hurt performance. Excess fertility results in overly lush growth and is likely to cause plants to lose their shape and flop unmanageably. This is true especially for highly nutrient-efficient genera, such as *Andropogon*, *Schizachyrium*, *Sorghastrum*, and *Miscanthus*.

Staking large grasses to hold them upright is particularly tedious and is usually unnecessary if fertility and water are kept to reasonable levels. Grasses that are specially adapted to infertile soils, such as broom-sedge, *Andropogon virginicus*, may lose their competitive edge and be overgrown by other plants if nutrient levels are raised significantly. Running grasses that are easily managed in average soils can become aggressive nuisances in overly rich soils. Also, the supergreen growth associated with high levels of fertility can diminish the vibrancy of foliage variegation.

Moisture

Drought tolerance is part of the natural appeal of ornamental grasses. Other than the watering of new transplants, reasonably situated ornamental grasses can do much to free gardeners from the waste and tedium of watering. Sometimes the challenge is how to deal with too much water in the garden. Grasses can often form part of the solution. Many of them do well in overly moist or even partly inundated soils. This is particularly true of sedges, rushes, cat-tails, and certain restios.

Diseases and Pests

Grasses are still among the most pest-free and disease-free of all garden ornamentals; however, a few problems have arrived along with the increased popularity of grasses. Not surprisingly, two of the most troublesome pests affect the ubiquitous miscanthus.

Miscanthus mealybug, *Miscanthicoccus miscanthi*, is a serious pest that fortunately appears to be restricted to the genus *Miscanthus*. An Asian native, it was first found in the United States in the late 1980s and is now in many northeastern states south to Florida and west to California. The mealybug cannot spread more than a few feet on its own. It has been dispersed unwittingly but entirely by the sale and exchange of infested plants.

The presence of this insidious pest is not usually noticed until the population on an individual plant builds to high levels and superficial symptoms become readily apparent. Up to $3/16$ in. (4 mm) long, the mealybug lives in the tight space between the stem and the enclosing leaf sheath. Colonies are usually established first toward the base (crown) of the plant and spread upward as their numbers increase. The mealybugs are difficult to see until they reach mature adult size. The best way to confirm their presence is to pull a lower leaf sheath away from the stem of an infested plant and look for the white, powdery wax and syrupy honeydew that is produced by and obscures the individual mealybugs.

Typically the first superficial symptoms are stunted growth and an uncharacteristic twisting in the flower heads. The stem and sheath tissue often turn dark red in areas where the mealybugs are feeding, especially in late season. Severely infested plants are not killed, but are reduced to unsightly, misshapen masses with white powder covering the stems, especially in the lower portion. Affected plants often fail to flower at all, or the stalks of the inflorescences may be stunted, causing the flowers to open down among the foliage rather than gracefully above.

Topical sprays are ineffective at eradicating the miscanthus mealybug, because they do not adequately penetrate the protected crevices between sheath and stem. Burning plants to the ground in spring and even scorching the crowns with a propane torch also fails to kill mealybugs that overwinter deep in the crown, near the soil line. To date, no natural predators have been found to be effective control agents. It is wisest to discard and incinerate infested plants and to check new miscanthus acquisitions carefully before adding them to the garden.

Miscanthus blight, described and identified by researchers at the USDA Agricultural Experiment Station in Maryland, is a foliar disease caused by *Stagonospora* and *Leptosphaeria* fungi. On mature plants, the blight is characterized by reddish brown spots or oval streaks on leaves and leaf sheaths. New leaf margins, tips, and older leaves become discolored and die. The disease can kill young seedlings and newly rooted cuttings. Fungicides can provide effective control.

Several grasses are susceptible to foliar rust diseases. Caused by fungi, rusts produce an orange or brownish discoloration on leaves. They are most likely to be a problem during warm, humid seasons, especially on cool-season grasses. Rusts can be avoided or minimized by planting susceptible grasses so that they have a maximum of air movement in warm periods and by overall good garden culture that minimizes plant stress. Rusts can be chemically controlled with applications of wettable sulfur or fungicides.

Deer rarely bother grasses. In fact, they do not like large grasses with sharp-edged leaves, and these can be used effectively to screen and protect other more vulnerable garden plants and areas. Gophers and voles, however, can be serious pests, devouring grass roots and killing or mangling the plants. These animals can be particularly disruptive to large groundcover plantings. Though unsightly, wire mesh coverings may be reasonably used to protect smaller numbers of plants from gophers.

Planting and Mulching Techniques

Generally, planting grasses is just like planting other garden perennials. The root systems of container-grown plants should be loosened before planting, and grasses should be thoroughly watered when planted and until they become established. Spring planting is suitable for most grasses, though cool-season growers often do well planted in autumn.

Grasses are sensitive to soil level, especially when young. Ideally, the crown of the grass should sit just slightly above the soil surface. Planting too low can rot grasses and planting too high can cause them to dry out and die.

Spacing of grasses has less to do with culture than design. Smaller grasses are relatively easy to transplant, so if the gardener's budget and energies allow, young plants can be spaced densely for quick effect and then rearranged as they attain a larger size. This approach is less practical with large grasses, which can require significant effort to move once established.

Grasses in native habitats are generally quite capable of establishing themselves in exposed soils; however, in the garden, mulch of all sorts can be an efficient method of controlling weeds and conserving soil moisture. Many species, such as the smaller fescues, *Festuca* species; the beard grasses, *Andropogon* species; and little bluestem, *Schizachyrium scoparium*, cannot tolerate having mulch pushed up around their crowns, a practice that often promotes rot and disease at the base of the plant. Mulching is most helpful to moisture-loving species, including many of the sedges and wood-rushes.

Young grass plants can be difficult to tell apart. Until one learns to recognize them reliably from their vegetative characters, it is wise to label plants or to sketch simple planting charts to record identities.

Responding to a gentle August breeze, plumes of *Calamagrostis ×acutiflora* 'Karl Foerster' bring movement to a courtyard in Washington State.

The powder-blue of *Leymus arenarius* plays off the weathered copper tones of a venerable vessel in early July in southern England.

The foliage color of *Carex elata* 'Aurea' is intensified by the moist, full-sun setting in this artful composition in England in early July.

Weeding

Keeping ornamental grasses free of weeds can be uniquely perplexing because the weeds are often unwanted grasses that can be difficult to distinguish from young plants of ornamental species. This is especially true when grasses are small and when they are not in flower. It pays to be diligent about removing weedy grasses at least until newly planted ornamentals have achieved some size and distinction. When attempting to distinguish weed grasses based on vegetative characters, look for differences in their ligules, leaf color, width, and general roughness, smoothness, or hairiness.

Even when ornamental grasses are mature, unwanted seedlings of other grasses sometimes germinate inside a clump. These should be pulled out by hand when they are noticed. It is easiest to do this when the soil is wet. If neglected for too long, weed seedlings can be impossible to remove unless the ornamental plant is lifted and divided.

Broad-leaf herbicides may be used around grasses; however, herbicides intended for weed grasses are often equally effective at eradicating ornamental species.

Cutting Back and Burning

Most grasses contribute years of beauty to the garden with little maintenance other than being cut back once a year. As a rule, late winter or early spring is the best time to cut back grasses, when the first signs of new growth are apparent.

Though gardening tradition commonly involves shearing everything to the ground as a means of "putting the garden neatly to bed" at the end of the growing season, this habit developed from a perception that the garden in winter had little to offer. Ornamental grasses are forcing a re-evaluation of this notion. Winter can truly be one of the peak seasons in gardens full of ornamental grasses and for this reason alone, spring cutting is more rewarding. Grasses left standing though the cold season do much to keep the garden alive and dynamic. They move with winter winds, they enhance the detail and beauty of frosts and snows, and they provide food and shelter for wildlife. From a purely practical standpoint, the stems and foliage from the past season often provide the crown of the grass with some protection from ice and cold.

Smaller grasses and a few larger ones may be easily trimmed back with hand pruners. Always wear gloves (at least on the hand opposite the pruning hand) to protect from cuts. A few grasses, including *Miscanthus*, have sharp leaf margins that can cause cuts to unprotected hands and faces. Manual hedge shears work well for trimming smaller grasses but are less precise than hand pruners. Electric hedge shears can make quick work of cutting back both large grasses and groundcover plantings of smaller species. An inexpensive bow saw can be a surprisingly efficient alternative to electric shears for cutting back large, thick-stemmed grasses. Power string trimmers and chain saws usually cause messy shattering and necessitate tedious cleanup.

Many evergreen grasses and sedges do not need to be cut back yearly and may grow attractively for several years with only minor grooming. One's fingers can be used to comb gently through the grasses and to pull out old or discolored foliage.

Though grasses in native habitats grow perfectly well without anyone to cut them back, they have often had the benefit of naturally occurring fires as a renewing agent. The efficacy of periodic firing of restored prairies and large meadow gardens is well proven; however, this potentially hazardous activity is best undertaken only by institutions and individuals with considerable safety support.

Small-scale controlled burning of ornamental grasses in residential gardens can be practical if proper caution is exercised and local burning ordinances are observed. Many grasses, especially *Miscanthus*, burn with surprising intensity. When burning grasses, choose a calm day in late winter or early spring and keep a watering hose within reach. Ensure that children and pets are at a safe distance, and also check grasses for active bird nests and beneficial insect egg cases. Do not attempt to burn grasses if they are close to shrubs or trees, especially conifers.

Side-lit by the waning, late October sun, *Panicum virgatum* 'Northwind' enlivens a naturalistic screen planting in the author's garden.

The neutral hues of *Bouteloua curtipendula* accentuate the richly colored gold *Rudbeckia nitida* and deep purple *Vernonia noveboracensis* in early August in Pennsylvania.

Dividing and Transplanting Techniques

Like many herbaceous perennials, older ornamental grasses may eventually begin to die at their centers and become unsightly and weak. Many can be easily renewed by division and transplanting. Grass plants made by division are best produced from the new outer growth, which is usually the strongest, healthiest material.

It is best to lift small and medium-sized grasses from the ground with a strong trowel or sharp spade and use a knife or narrow-edged trowel to divide them. Discard dead material from the center and thoroughly water divisions immediately following transplanting.

A sharp sturdy spade, not a shovel, is essential for dividing and managing the largest grasses. Mature specimens are often too big and heavy to be lifted in one piece and must be sectioned in the ground with a spade before they can be lifted. Unless one is working around buried electrical lines, the best type of spade is one constructed entirely of modern steel alloys, which are light but exceptionally strong. Some manufacturers offer spades with cushioning rubber footpads at the top of the blade. This type of tool is comfortable to use when cutting into the roots of grasses and is strong enough to be used to lever heavy divisions out of the ground. In situations where electrical lines may be present, only spades insulated with nonconducting materials should be used.

The author's garden in early November is saturated with the rich tones of switchgrass, *Panicum virgatum* 'Northwind' (left), and Lindheimer's muhly, *Muhlenbergia lindheimeri*, set against a cut-leaf form of smooth sumac, *Rhus glabra*.

ORNAMENTAL GRASSES
FOR SPECIFIC PURPOSES AND LOCATIONS

The lists that follow are representative only and do not include every ornamental grass described in this guide. Gardeners are encouraged to be creative in their use of ornamental grasses in the landscape.

Clumping Ornamental Grasses

Achnatherum
Andropogon
Briza media
Calamagrostis
Carex grayi
Carex lupulina
Carex pendula
Carex testacea
Chasmanthium latifolium
Cortaderia richardii
Cyperus papyrus
Deschampsia cespitosa
Elymus
Eragrostis
Festuca glauca
Holcus lanatus
Miscanthus 'Giganteus'
Miscanthus 'Purpurascens'
Miscanthus sinensis
Molinia
Muhlenbergia lindheimeri
Nassella
Panicum virgatum
Pennisetum 'Burgundy Giant'
Pennisetum orientale
Pennisetum setaceum
Poa colensoi
Saccharum ravennae
Spartina bakeri
Sporobolus airoides
Stipa
Themeda
Tridens

Running Ornamental Grasses

Ammophila
Arundo
Buchloe dactyloides
Carex flacca
Carex montana
Carex morrowii
Carex riparia 'Variegata'
Chondropetalum tectorum
Eleocharis dulcis
Festuca rubra
Glyceria maxima
Hakonechloa
Hierochloe
Imperata
Juncus
Luzula
Miscanthus sacchariflorus
Muhlenbergia dumosa
Panicum amarum
Pennisetum incomptum
Phalaris
Phragmites
Saccharum giganteum
Spartina pectinata 'Aureomarginata'
Stenotaphrum
Tripsacum dactyloides

Cool-Season Ornamental Grasses

Achnatherum
Briza
Carex
Deschampsia
Festuca
Hakonechloa macra
Koeleria glauca
Melica
Milium effusum
Phalaris arundinacea
Stipa

Warm-Season Ornamental Grasses

Andropogon gerardii
Arundo donax
Chasmanthium latifolium

Opposite: *Arundo donax* flowering in late October in Pennsylvania.

23

Cortaderia
Elymus
Miscanthus
Molinia
Panicum virgatum
Pennisetum
Saccharum ravennae
Sorghastrum nutans

Ornamental Grasses for Groundcover

Alopecurus pratensis 'Variegatus'
Bouteloua gracilis
Carex morrowii var. morrowii
Chasmanthium latifolium
Festuca
Hakonechloa macra
Holcus mollis
Leymus arenarius
Pennisetum alopecuroides 'Hameln'
Phalaris arundinacea
Sesleria
Sporobolus heterolepis

Ornamental Grasses for Mass Planting

Andropogon virginicus
Bouteloua curtipendula
Calamagrostis brachytricha
Melica ciliata
Muhlenbergia capillaris
Panicum virgatum
Pennisetum alopecuroides
Spodiopogon sibiricus
Themeda japonica
Tridens flavus

Ornamental Grasses for Specimen Planting

Arundo donax
Calamagrostis ×acutiflora 'Karl Foerster'
Festuca californica
Helictotrichon sempervirens
Muhlenbergia capillaris
Panicum virgatum
Pennisetum orientale
Phalaris arundinacea
Spodiopogon sibiricus
Themeda japonica

Ornamental Grasses for Cut Flowers

Achnatherum calamagrostis
Andropogon ternarius
Briza media
Calamagrostis ×acutiflora 'Karl Foerster'
Cymophyllus fraserianus
Eriophorum
Miscanthus
Pennisetum
Sorghastrum nutans
Stipa gigantea
Zizania aquatica

Ornamental Grasses for Screening

Andropogon gerardii
Arundo donax
Calamagrostis ×acutiflora 'Karl Foerster'
Panicum amarum
Panicum virgatum

Ornamental Grasses for Movement in Breezes

Briza media
Calamagrostis ×acutiflora 'Karl Foerster'
Chondropetalum tectorum
Hesperostipa spartea
Molinia caerulea subsp. arundinacea
Nassella tenuissima
Stipa gigantea

Ornamental Grasses for Water Gardens

Dulichium arundinaceum
Rhynchospora
Schoenoplectus
Typha minima
Zizania

Ornamental Grasses for the Edge of Water

Carex spissa
Cortaderia richardii Cyperus
Cyperus
Glyceria maxima 'Variegata'
Isolepis cernua
Juncus
Miscanthus 'Giganteus'
Miscanthus sinensis 'Morning Light'

Panicum virgatum
Phragmites australis 'Variegatus'
Schoenoplectus tabernaemontani
Scirpus

Ornamental Grasses for Dry Sites

Andropogon
Buchloe dactyloides
Carex flacca
Cortaderia selloana
Eragrostis elliottii
Leymus arenarius
Luzula sylvatica
Muhlenbergia rigens
Nassella tenuissima
Sesleria
Sporobolus heterolepis
Themeda japonica

Ornamental Grasses for Containers

Calamagrostis brachytricha
Carex phyllocephala 'Sparkler'
Chasmanthium latifolium
Cortaderia selloana 'Aureolineata'
Elymus magellanicus
Festuca glauca
Miscanthus sinensis 'Morning Light'
Muhlenbergia dumosa
Pennisetum alopecuroides
Phragmites australis 'Variegatus'
Typha latifolia 'Variegata'
Vetiveria zizanoides

Evergreen Ornamental Grasses in Milder Climates

Alopecurus pratensis 'Variegatus'
Carex
Cortaderia selloana
Deschampsia cespitosa
Eragrostis curvula
Festuca californica
Festuca mairei
Helictotrichon sempervirens
Luzula
Merxmuellera macowanii
Nassella tenuissima
Stipa gigantea
Uncinia

Ornamental Grasses for Woodlands

Carex siderosticha
Luzula
Milium
Saccharum alopecuroidum

Ornamental Grasses for Dry Shade

Chasmanthium latifolium
Deschampsia flexuosa
Hystrix patula

Ornamental Grasses for Fragrance

Cymbopogon citratus
Hierochloe
Sporobolus heterolepis

Ornamental Grasses for Clay Soil

Andropogon hallii 'Silver Sunrise'
Andropogon ternarius
Calamagrostis ×*acutiflora* 'Karl Foerster'
Luzula sylvatica
Saccharum contortum
Sorghastrum nutans
Sporobolus airoides

Ornamental Grasses for Sandy Soil

Andropogon hallii 'Silver Sunrise'
Sporobolus airoides

Ornamental Grasses for Acid Soil

Briza media
Carex caryophyllea
Eleocharis acicularis
Eriophorum
Holcus mollis
Luzula sylvatica
Molinia caerulea
Schizachyrium scoparium
Schoenoplectus tabernaemontani

Ornamental Grasses for Alkaline Soil

Carex montana
Leymus
Molinia caerulea
Schizachyrium scoparium
Sesleria
Sporobolus airoides

Salt-tolerant Ornamental Grasses

Ammophila
Calamagrostis nutkaensis
Hordeum
Leymus arenarius
Spartina pectinata

Ornamental Grasses with Yellow-striped Leaves

Alopecurus pratensis 'Variegatus'
Bromis inermis 'Skinner's Gold'
Carex elata 'Aurea'
Carex oshimensis 'Evergold'
Cortaderia selloana 'Aureolineata'
Cortaderia selloana 'Monvin'
Glyceria maxima 'Variegata'
Juncus effusus 'Cuckoo'
Miscanthus sinensis 'Goldfeder'
Molinia caerulea 'Variegata'
Phalaris arundinacea 'Luteopicta'
Phragmites australis 'Variegatus'
Schizachyrium scoparium 'Stars & Stripes'

Ornamental Grasses with White-striped Leaves

Arrhenatherum elatius subsp. bulbosum 'Variegatum'
Arundo donax 'Variegata'
Calamagrostis ×acutiflora 'Overdam'
Carex ornithopoda 'Variegata'
Carex riparia 'Variegata'
Carex siderosticha 'Variegata'
Cortaderia selloana 'Albolineata'
Cortaderia selloana 'Silver Comet'
Cyperus alternifolius 'Variegatus'
Deschampsia cespitosa 'Northern Lights'
Hakonechloa macra 'Albovariegata'
Holcus mollis 'Variegatus'
Miscanthus sinensis 'Variegatus'
Pennisetum alopecuroides 'Little Honey'
Phalaris arundinacea 'Feesey'
Phalaris arundinacea 'Picta'
Stenotaphrum secundatum 'Variegatum'
Typha latifolia 'Variegata'

Ornamental Grasses for Fall Color

Achnatherum calamagrostis
Andropogon
Anemanthele lessoniana

Bothriochloa saccharoides
Bouteloua curtipendula
Chasmanthium latifolium
Hakonechloa macra
Miscanthus sinensis 'Adagio'
Molinia caerulea
Muhlenbergia lindheimeri Autumn Glow™
Panicum virgatum
Pennisetum alopecuroides
Spodiopogon sibiricus
Sporobolus airoides
Tridens flavus
Typha
Vetiveria zizanoides

Ornamental Grasses with Blue Foliage

Andropogon capillipes
Andropogon hallii
Calamagrostis foliosa
Elymus magellanicus
Festuca amethystina 'Superba'
Festuca californica
Festuca glauca 'Elijah Blue'
Festuca idahoensis
Helictotrichon sempervirens
Juncus inflexus 'Lovesick Blues'
Leymus arenarius
Panicum amarum 'Dewey Blue'
Poa colensoi
Sesleria caerulea
Sorghastrum nutans 'Sioux Blue'

Ornamental Grasses with Purple Foliage

Saccharum officinarum 'Violaceum'

Ornamental Grasses with Reddish Foliage

Chionochloa rubra
Imperata cylindrica var. koenigii 'Red Baron'
Uncinia

Ornamental Grasses with Gray-Green Foliage

Arundo donax
Bouteloua curtipendula
Festuca mairei
Leymus cinereus
Panicum virgatum 'Dallas Blues'

Ornamental Grasses with Brown Foliage

Carex buchananii
Carex comans
Hakonechloa macra 'Beni Fuchi'

Ornamental Grasses with Yellowish Foliage

Deschampsia flexuosa 'Aurea'
Festuca glauca 'Golden Toupee'
Glyceria obtusa
Milium effusum 'Aureum'

Overleaf: *Miscanthus* 'Purpurascens' fall foliage in full sun in early October in Pennsylvania.

ACHNATHERUM
Needle grass (Grass family)

Comprised of densely tufted, clump-forming species from central and southern Europe, eastern Asia, and western North America. The common name alludes to the numerous awns on the florets, a characteristic *Achnatherum* shares with *Stipa* and one that contributes to the feathery, luminescent qualities of the inflorescences. Most species are cool-season growers, freely flowering in spring or early summer and often remaining attractive for months. They are most beautiful in areas with strong summer sun but cool nights and low humidity.

Achnatherum calamagrostis
Silver spike grass

Native to high-elevation clearings in central and southern Europe. One of the most graceful, free-flowering medium-sized ornamental grasses if provided plenty of sunlight, low humidity, and cool summer nights (unmanageably floppy elsewhere or if grown in more than light shade). Clump-forming and densely tufted. Produces a fountain of refined, medium-green foliage topped in June or July by full but equally fine-textured silver-green inflorescences. To 3 ft. (1 m) tall in bloom. The flowers turn beautifully tawny by August and remain attractive throughout winter in milder climates. They make excellent cut material. The foliage turns mostly yellow in autumn, remaining slightly evergreen in mild climates and going fully dormant in colder regions. Grows best in well-drained soil with even moisture and low to average fertility. Showy enough for specimen use, also superb in drifts and sweeps. Propagate by seed or by division in spring. Zone 5.

'Lemperg'. Slightly more compact than the type. Propagate by division.

Mature plants of *Achnatherum calamagrostis* are dramatic in plantings in Germany in late August.

29

Achnatherum coronatum in early July in California.

Achnatherum hymenoides is side-lit by the mid-June sun in California.

Achnatherum speciosum adds rich tans and browns to the early February landscape in California.

Achnatherum coronatum
Needle grass

Native to dry, sunny, gravelly, rocky slopes and chaparral areas at elevations to 5000 ft. (1500 m), mostly in southern California. Flowers in spring, on upright culms 3–6 ft. (1–2 m) tall. Tufted, leaves mostly basal. Attractive and especially suited to sunny, dry sites. Propagate by seed. Zone 8.

Achnatherum hymenoides
Indian rice grass, sand grass

Native to northern Mexico and from California to British Columbia on well-drained or sandy soils in desert shrublands, sagebrush, and pinyon/juniper woodlands, this delicate, airy grass has suffered from severe habitat destruction due to cattle grazing. Fine textured, to 2 ft. (60 cm) tall, it is a cool-season grower, producing attractive, open flower panicles in early spring and going dormant

Achnatherum speciosum in mid-June in California.

for summer. Grows well in extremely dry situations. Will succumb to excess moisture. Propagate by seed. Zone 8.

Achnatherum speciosum
Desert needle grass
Native to desert communities from California to Colorado south to Mexico and South America, this long-lived grass can get by on 5–10 in. (12–25 cm) annual rainfall. The extremely fine foliage forms a rounded basal tuft that turns from gray-green in spring and summer to rich tans and light browns in winter. Narrow flower panicles appear in early spring and remain fluffy into summer. Makes a great textural foil for bold cacti and other desert succulents. Propagate by seed. Zone 8.

Achnatherum splendens
Chee grass
Native to steppes and semidesert sands, gravels, stony slopes, and alkaline areas in central Asia and Siberia, sometimes forming the basis of large vegetation groups known as chee grass associations. This stately grass can reach 8 ft. (2.4 m) tall in flower. It blooms in June to July, producing open, feathery, purplish pink panicles held high on slender stalks above a large basal mound of slightly gray-green narrow foliage. The inflorescences fade to tan but remain intact and attractive. A true cool-season grower that likes full sun but needs lower nighttime temperatures. A magnificent specimen or focal point. Semi-evergreen in milder climates. Best propagated by seed. Zone 7.

Achnatherum splendens at flowering peak in mid-July in England.

ALOPECURUS
Foxtail grass (Grass family)

The genus name means "fox tail," referring to the soft, cylindrical flower panicles. Comprised of nearly 30 annual and perennial species native to northern temperate regions and temperate South America. Most are meadow and pasture species of little ornamental value. The Eurasian native *A. pratensis* has naturalized over much of North America. It forms dense tufts of solid green leaves to 3 ft. (1 m) tall in flower and spreads slowly by rhizomes. A cool-season grower, it is nearly evergreen in mild temperate climates. Only its variegated form is ornamentally significant.

Alopecurus pratensis 'Variegatus'
Variegated foxtail grass

Also called 'Aureovariegatus' or 'Aureus'. Among the most colorful yellow-leaved grasses. Has a flowering height of only 2 ft. (60 cm). The narrow leaves vary from bright green with vivid yellow longitudinal stripes to nearly solid yellow, producing an overall golden effect, especially when backlit or side-lit. Yellow color is most intense when plants are grown in full sun, although half-shaded plantings are still a pleasing chartreuse. Nearly evergreen in mild temperate climates. Flowers in late April or May are of minimal ornamental value. To retain foliage color in summer, cut plants back to about 5 in. (12 cm) when flowering begins. If uncut, the flowers and foliage become unsightly by July or August. Colorful, new growth resumes in cooler weather, and plants remain attractive until temperatures drop to freezing. A reliable performer of easy culture, tolerant of a wide range of soil types and moisture conditions. Effective as a color accent or in large groundcover sweeps. Propagate by division in spring or fall; the variegation does not come true from seed. Zone 4.

Alopecurus pratensis 'Variegatus' brightens the mossy edge of a path in Washington State in mid-May.

AMMOPHILA
Beach grass, dune grass (Grass family)

The genus name means "sand loving," referring to the preferred habitat. Comprised of two species of coarse, strongly rhizomatous warm-season grasses, one native to coastal Europe and northern Africa, the other to coastal North America. In their native regions, both play critical roles in the stabilization of coastal dunes. New shoots produced from the rhizomes allow these grasses to survive burial by shifting dune sands. Both are salt tolerant. Selected forms are usually propagated by division and planted 1 ft. (30 cm) deep.

Ammophila arenaria
European beach grass

Native to coastal Europe and northern Africa. The species epithet means "of the sand." This aggressively running species has been widely employed for erosion control in dunes and other sandy soils. Inappropriate introduction to the West Coast of North America has resulted in the displacement of native dune species, and *A. arenaria* is there considered an invasive exotic. Zone 5.

Ammophila breviligulata
American beach grass

Native to coastal North America and essential to the visual character and environmental health of sandy beaches and dunes. Although wind and salt tolerant, it cannot withstand regular foot traffic. Cultivars based on provenance are available for different regions. Plant divisions anytime from mid-October to mid-April, except when ground is frozen. Do not plant in summer. Zone 5.

'Cape'. A superior selection from Cape Cod, Massachusetts. Performs best from Maine south through the mid-Atlantic states.

'Hatteras'. Performs better than 'Cape' in southern areas.

ANDROPOGON
Beard grass (Grass family)

The genus name refers to the silky hairs on the flower spikelets of some species. Comprised of approximately 100 species of annual and perennial grasses native from tropical regions to temperate North America. The important ornamental

Ammophila breviligulata stabilizes New Jersey dunes in mid-July.

species are all clump-forming, warm-season North American natives. Most flower in late summer and enliven autumn and winter landscapes with rich, long-lasting orange, red, and copper colors. All are deciduous and are best cut back in late winter or early spring. Propagate by seed or by division in spring.

Andropogon capillipes
Blue beard grass, chalky bluestem

Grows naturally on dry sandy pine barrens from Florida to Mississippi and north into southeastern Virginia. Similar in most respects to broom-sedge, *A. virginicus*, and considered synonymous by some botanists. Horticulturally, it is often quite distinct in having slightly wider, strongly glaucous-blue summer foliage. Upright in stature, usually 2–3 ft. (60–90 cm) tall. Blooms mid-September to early October. Prefers full sun and does best on sharply drained soils of low to average fertility. Very drought tolerant but not as cold

hardy as broom-sedge. Zone 7, but very heat tolerant, thriving into zone 10.

'Silver Beauty'. Leaves silver-blue in summer, picking up purplish tones in autumn.

'Valdosta Blue'. Leaves chalky-blue in summer, picking up purplish tones in autumn. Selected from a native population growing near Valdosta, Georgia.

Andropogon gerardii
Big bluestem, turkey foot

Grows on moist and dry soils, in prairies and open woods, from central Mexico throughout much of the United States and into Canada. A regal species referred to as the monarch of the prairie grasses. The tallest North American member of the genus, it grows 5–8 ft. (1.5–2.4 m) tall. Upright and strictly clump-forming, leaves to 3/8 in. (9 mm) wide, green or blue-green in summer, reliably turning rich orange and copper-red in autumn, sometimes with deep

Andropogon capillipes 'Silver Beauty' in mid-September in Virginia.

Andropogon gerardii beginning to flower in mid-August in southern Germany.

Andropogon gerardii 'Sentinel' beginning to bloom in late July in eastern Pennsylvania.

Tiny red anthers hang from threadlike filaments and feathery pink stigmas in big bluestem, *Andropogon gerardii*.

burgundy tints. Terminal inflorescences appear in late August or early September, opening red and turning darker with age, three-parted and vaguely resembling an upside-down turkey foot. They are interesting but not showy. The main appeal of this grass is its lush summer foliage and fall and winter color. In the garden, the size and upright stature can be quite dramatic. Ideal for deciduous screening, naturalizing, meadow gardens, and prairie restorations. Will grow lax and floppy if shaded. Adapted to a wide range of soil and moisture conditions. Propagate by seed or by division in spring. A sturdy, long-lived grass. Zone 3.

'Sentinel'. A remarkably sturdy, upright, blue-green selection. To 7 ft. (2.1 m) tall in flower. Zone 3.

Andropogon glomeratus
Bushy beard grass
Inhabits low, moist ground, marshes, and swamps in the eastern coastal United States. Typically 2–4 ft. (60–120 cm) tall, but sometimes taller. Foliage to ⅜ in. (9 mm) wide, green in summer, turning copper-orange in autumn. Flowers in September, enclosed in densely clustered bushy bracts at the top of the stems. Flowering stems very attractive on the plant and in cut or dried arrangements. Differs from most other Andropogon species in this book in its preference for moist or nearly wet sites. Grows in garden soils of average moisture, but is not drought tolerant. Full sun to very light shade. Sturdy and upright, retaining its fall color long through winter. Propagate by seed or by division in spring. Zone 5.

Andropogon gyrans
Elliott's broom-sedge
Found on dry or moist fields and open woods in the eastern states, often with broom-sedge, A. virginicus, from which it differs in having the inflorescences clustered at the upper portion of the stem, surrounded by broad, showy sheaths. Green in summer, the culms and sheaths turn vivid orange in late autumn and winter, and are

Andropogon glomeratus growing native in coastal New Jersey in mid-October.

Andropogon gyrans in early January in Pennsylvania.

Andropogon hallii 'Silver Sunrise' in late September in trials in Nebraska.

Andropogon ternarius in late November in the author's Pennsylvania garden.

quite striking. Stands through repeated snows. Strictly clump-forming, 2–3 ft. (60–90 cm) tall. Best in groups, sweeps, or meadow gardens in full sun or very light shade. Drought tolerant. Grows on poor soils. Cut stems suitable for dry arrangements. Does not tolerate heavy mulch at base. Propagate by seed or by division in spring. Zone 5.

Andropogon hallii
Hall's bluestem, sand bluestem
Native to sandhills and dry plains from Montana to Utah and southeast to Texas, this species looks much like big bluestem, *A. gerardii*, except that the foliage is a distinct chalky-blue. It is also more drought tolerant. Best in full sun on sandy soils, typically reaching 5–6 ft. (1.5–2 m). Little known in gardens, but deserving of much greater attention. Zone 3.

'Champ'. A hybrid between *A. gerardii* and *A. hallii*, developed by Lawrence Newell at the Uni-

versity of Nebraska, Lincoln, and selected for its adaptability to a variety of soil types.

'Silver Sunrise'. This new introduction from the Great Plants for the Great Plains program is exceptionally upright in habit, with stunning blue-gray summer foliage and strong purple tints in late autumn. Prominent yellow bands are increasingly noticeable as the season progresses, adding significantly to the appeal of this cultivar. Grows well in sand or clay soils, but is most upright in drier conditions. To 6 ft. (2 m) tall in flower. Zone 3.

Andropogon ternarius
Split-beard broom-sedge
Native from southern Delaware, often on sandy soils along the coastal plain to Florida and Texas, but also on clay soils from Georgia to Missouri. Similar enough to *A. virginicus* to be mistaken for it until the flowers appear, held out from the stems on conspicuous slender stalks. Inflores-

cences very silvery when dry, especially attractive when back-lit. Summer foliage often glaucous blue-green, turning shades of purple-bronze, copper, and red in fall. A beautiful, underappreciated grass worth growing for cut flowers alone, especially dried. Full sun. Drought tolerant. Does not tolerate heavy mulch at base. Propagate by seed or by division in spring. Zone 6.

Andropogon virginicus
Beard grass, broom-sedge

Ranges over much of North America on open ground, old fields, and sterile hills, on dense or sandy soils. Upright, strictly clump-forming, to 4 ft. (1.2 m) tall in flower. Stems and leaves green in summer, suffused dark red-purple when flowers first appear in September, turning bright orange in late fall, the color persisting through winter and into the following spring. Inflorescences attractively silver when back-lit. Rarely noticed in summer, this grass is primarily responsible (along with little bluestem, *Schizachyrium scoparium*) for the tawny-orange winter color of many old fields and pastures. Stunning in vast sweeps. Not

Andropogon virginicus in late October in Pennsylvania.

Andropogon virginicus in sweeps along a Georgia highway embankment in late January.

for the formal garden, but a fine addition to meadow gardens, natural areas, highway medians, and embankments. Requires full sun and is longest lived on relatively infertile soils. Extremely drought tolerant. Does not tolerate heavy mulch at base. Propagate by seed or by division in spring. Zone 3.

ANEMANTHELE
New Zealand wind grass (Grass family)
Comprised of a single species native to New Zealand. Split from *Stipa*.

Anemanthele lessoniana
Pheasant's-tail grass
This New Zealand endemic grows at the edges of small streams at elevations to 1500 ft. (640 m). Rarely grown outside its home country and England, it deserves wider attention. Forms a dense tussock of arching, fine-textured, semi-evergreen foliage that is medium green in summer, with various gold and orange tints appearing in autumn and winter. In early summer, slight feathery inflorescences arch outward just above the leaves, to 3

ft. (1 m). Flower and foliage colors best in full sun, but tolerate partial shade. Propagate by seed or by division in spring. Zone 7b.

'Autumn Tints'. Leaves flushed deep red-orange in late summer.

'Gold Hue'. Leaves flushed gold in late summer.

ARISTIDA
Three-awn (Grass family)
Comprised of approximately 300 species of bunchgrasses native to warmer, usually arid parts of the world. A few species are noxious weeds.

Aristida purpurea
Purple three-awn
Native to dry areas across the North American plains and into northern Mexico. Quite variable and often segregated into numerous botanical varieties. Foliage green or sometimes glaucous-blue. Erect-growing, to 2½ ft. (80 cm) tall. Flowers strongly red or tinted purple. A beautiful component of dry grasslands, especially when the conspicuous long awns catch the autumn light. Smaller groupings can enhance arid-region gar-

Anemanthele lessoniana in flower in early July in England.

Aristida purpurea adds red tints in early July to a California meadow.

dens, but self-sowing can be a nuisance. Full sun. Does not tolerate moist conditions. Propagates easily by seed. Zone 6.

ARRHENATHERUM
Oat grass (Grass family)

Comprised of six perennial species in Europe, Africa, and Asia, only one of which is grown ornamentally. The European native *A. elatius* subsp. *bulbosum*, tuber oat grass, can be invasive; it produces conspicuous bulbous storage organs at the base of the stems, which root readily to produce new plants. It has green leaves and is rarely cultivated for ornament; however, its variegated cultivar is well behaved and is among the brightest whites of all the grasses.

Arrhenatherum elatius subsp. *bulbosum* 'Variegatum'
Striped tuber oat grass

Clear white longitudinal stripes dominate dark green leaves, so that the plant appears nearly all white from a few feet away. This cool-season grower is stunning in climates with dry summers

Arrhenatherum elatius subsp. *bulbosum* 'Variegatum' in late May with *Brunnera macrophylla* 'Langtrees'.

and cool nights, where it produces a neat mound of spreading foliage to 1 ft. (30 cm) tall, remaining attractive into winter. In humid, hot areas where night temperatures remain high, it is often afflicted with foliar rust diseases by midsummer, becoming very unattractive and often going completely dormant. Partial shade minimizes summer stress and does not affect intensity of variegation. New foliage appears in fall, and the plants are again beautiful going into winter. Mildly attractive flowers produced on upright stems in summer only in cooler climates. To remain vigorous and attractive needs frequent division, best in spring or fall. An excellent subject for display in pots. Zone 3.

ARUNDO
Reed (Grass family)

Comprised of three species, all strongly rhizomatous, warm-season growers native mostly to damp places and riverbanks from the Mediterranean region to eastern Asia. The genus name means "reed."

Arundo donax
Giant reed

Long a source of reeds for wind instruments, this native of the Mediterranean region grows larger and taller than any other grass hardy in cool temperate regions, excepting the bamboos. In the northeastern United States, where it dies to the ground each winter, it can attain 14 ft. (4.2 m) in a single season. It may reach 18 ft. (5.5 m) in warm regions where it remains evergreen.

Stems upright, leaves coarse, gray-green, to 3 in. (7.5 cm) wide. Strongly spreading by thick rhizomes. At summer's end, 1-ft. (0.3-m) inflorescences top the culms, opening with a pink cast and drying to silver. They are dramatic in the landscape and in dried arrangements. Requires a long warm season for flower production, but worth growing in other areas for the bold stems and leaves. E. A. Bowles called it "the king of grasses for foliage effect." Cut back in late autumn.

Striking as a specimen or screen planting. Young plants are ideal container specimens. Not

Arundo donax 'Variegata' in mid-June in Pennsylvania.

Arundo plinii in research trials in Pennsylvania in early November.

particular as to soils or fertility. Tolerates drought tolerant and periodic standing water. Sets fertile seed only in warm climates, such as southern California, and there it has become a serious invader of moist native habitats.

Old, established specimens require considerable effort to divide, transplant, or remove due to sheer weight and size. Fortunately, the rhizomes are relatively soft, and a sharp spade easily cuts through them. Propagates easily by rooting rhizome pieces. Best divided in spring. Zone 6.

'Variegata' ('Versicolor'). Striped giant reed. Leaves and stems dramatically striped cream-white. Variegation is brightest white during cool springs, becomes cream-yellow with warmth, and may fade to yellow-green by end of a hot summer. Shorter and more tender than the species. Flowers infrequently. Stunning when grown in a pot. Zone 6.

Arundo plinii

A native of the Mediterranean region similar to but smaller in all its parts than *A. donax*, more re-sembling *Phragmites communis*. Attractive, flowering in late summer, but has proved a tenacious runner in trials at Longwood Gardens, and can only be recommended for planting where it will be well contained. An unnamed bluish green form with sharp narrow leaves is often offered commercially. It may represent a semi-permanent juvenile type of growth. It is equally aggressive. Zone 6.

AUSTROSTIPA
Australian feather grass (Grass family)
A genus segregated from *Stipa* and comprised entirely of Australian natives.

Austrostipa ramosissima
Australian plume grass, pillar of smoke
Grows to 8 ft. (2.4 m) in moist, well-drained gullies near the edges of forests or woods in its native Australia, flowering most of the year in response to rains. The name pillar of smoke is apt. Upright and clump-forming, this grass blooms nearly continuously in cultivation, producing a dense,

towering mass of fine-textured inflorescences. Propagates readily by seed. Zone 8, possibly colder.

BOTHRIOCHLOA
Grass family
Comprised of approximately 28 warm-season species. Sometimes included in *Andropogon*.

Bothriochloa saccharoides
Silver beard grass, silver bluestem
Native to prairies, plains, and dry, open places over much of the central and southwestern United States. Forms upright clumps 3–4 ft. (90–120 cm) tall. Named for the small but conspicuous silver inflorescences, held on slender stalks branching from the stems. Blooms spring into fall. Leaves medium green. Similar in overall appearance to *Andropogon ternarius* and, though not as showy, better adapted to hot drier regions. Foliage turns orange and red in autumn, remaining colorful into winter. Zone 5.

BOUTELOUA
Grama, grama grass (Grass family)
Named for Spanish botanist brothers Claudio and Esteban Boutelou. Comprised of approximately 30 annual and perennial species native to dry open grasslands in the Americas, from Canada to Argentina. Two are the predominant species of the North American shortgrass prairie (also called the Great Plains), a region that is drier than the tallgrass prairie. Both species are clump-forming, warm-season growers with considerable cold hardiness. They are quite distinct in flowering appearance.

Bouteloua curtipendula
Side-oats grama
Native from eastern Canada to California and south to Argentina. The common name refers to the oatlike spikelets, which are held mostly to one side of the inflorescences. The numerous inflorescences arch above the basal mound of gray-green foliage, to a height of 3 ft. (1 m), and are purplish when they first appear in June or July. Continually produced through most of the sum-

Austrostipa ramosissima in mid-December in California.

mer, they bleach to a straw color as they age. Autumn foliage colors include bronze-purple, orange, and red. Requires full sun, but tolerates a range of soils and prolonged drought. Cut back in late autumn. Most effective in mass plantings or groupings, especially against contrasting background. A fine addition to a meadow garden but overwhelmed by other grasses in moist settings. Propagates readily by seed or by division in spring. Zone 4.

Bouteloua gracilis
Blue grama, mosquito grass
Found mostly on dry plains from Wisconsin to Manitoba south to southern California and Texas. Usually only 8–15 in. (20–38 cm) tall in full flower, this diminutive grass produces its curious inflorescences in June through September, suspended horizontally like tiny brushes from the tip of each flowering stem. They are strongly red-tinted at first, bleaching to a straw color. Best in a sunny garden

The one-sided inflorescences of *Bouteloua curtipendula* in early August in Pennsylvania.

A mass planting of *Bouteloua curtipendula* in a German garden.

Bouteloua gracilis in mid-September in Maryland.

Bouteloua gracilis makes an attractive water-conserving lawn in late August in Colorado.

spot near a path, on top of a ledge, or in a decorative container, where its detail can be appreciated. Can also be planted densely and mowed to 2 in. (5 cm) to provide a water-conserving lawn or groundcover in dry areas. Propagate by seed. Self-sows but is easily managed. Zone 3.

BRIZA
Quaking grass (Grass family)

Comprised of 20 annual and perennial species native to grasslands in temperate Eurasia and South America, and widely introduced elsewhere for their ornamental flower spikelets.

Briza media
Common quaking grass, rattle grass

This Eurasian native is common nearly throughout the British Isles on a variety of soils from light to heavy, dry to damp, and acid to calcareous. A cool-season grower. Diffusely branched inflorescences appear in May and are tipped with pendent spikelets resembling puffy oats. To 2½ ft. (80 cm)

tall, these are conspicuously attractive in the landscape, rattling and rustling delightfully in spring and summer breezes. They also make superb cut flowers. At first green with tints of red-purple, they bleach to a light straw color by midsummer. Cutting them at various stages preserves the different colors. Clump-forming, producing a dense tuft of soft, deep green, fine-textured foliage that is semi-evergreen even in cold climates. No appreciable fall color. Reliable and easy to grow in full sun or even partial shade. Remove inflorescences in late summer and shear foliage lightly to encourage a new flush of autumn growth that remains attractive into winter. Durable and long-lived. Sweeps and masses planted for flower effect also double as groundcovers. Zone 4.

BROMUS
Brome, chess (Grass family)

Comprised of approximately 100 species, mostly native to northern temperate regions. The genus name means "oat."

Briza media in early July in Pennsylvania.

Bromus inermis 'Skinner's Gold' in mid-July in North Carolina.

Bromus inermis
Smooth brome

A perennial with creeping rhizomes. Native to Europe, Siberia, Mongolia, and Manchuria. Naturalized in the western United States, where it is often used as a hay and pasture grass. Of ornamental importance for the following variegated cultivar.

'Skinner's Gold'. Skinner's gold brome. Leaves mostly green-margined with broad, light yellow longitudinal variegation. Flower stalks also yellow, giving a light yellow overall appearance to the plant. To 3 ft. (1 m) tall in flower in midsummer. Propagate by division in spring. Zone 3.

BUCHLOE
Buffalo grass (Grass family)

The genus name is shortened from *bubalochloe* (buffalo grass). Comprised of a single perennial species native to the North American Great Plains as far north as Montana and south into Mexico. Ornamental in that it is a water-conserving, fuel-conserving alternate to typical lawn grasses.

Buchloe dactyloides
Buffalo grass

A strongly stoloniferous warm-season grower. Naturally drought tolerant and only 4–8 in. (10–20 cm) tall at maturity. Deciduous, growing blue-green through warmer seasons and turning golden brown in winter dormancy. Returns to green earlier in spring than St. Augustine grass or Bermuda grass, and its texture is much finer, more welcoming to bare feet. Withstands considerable foot traffic. Among a minority of dioecious grasses, having male and female flowers on separate plants. May be grown from seed, which produces a mix of male and female plants; however, selections for lawn use are often vegetatively propagated female clones that provide a more uniform appearance. Female plants are also pollen-free. Does best in sun on heavy soils. Does not tolerate constant moisture. Of proven

Calamagrostis ×*acutiflora* 'Karl Foerster' contrasts with *Eryngium oliverianum* in early July in England.

performance in the southwestern United States and showing promise for other areas, including the Northeast. Cultivars are being developed for best performance in various regions. **'Prairie'** and **'609'** grow to 8 in. (20 cm) tall if unmowed. **'Cody'** and **'Tatanka'** are even shorter. Zone 4.

CALAMAGROSTIS
Reed grass (Grass family)

The genus name means "reed grass." Comprised of 250 perennial species mostly native to moist areas, including wet woodlands, alpine meadows, beaches, and coastal marshes in northern temperate regions. Plants produce many natural hybrids. Though the Eurasian species are most often seen in gardens, the many beautiful western American natives deserve to be better known.

Calamagrostis ×acutiflora
Feather reed grass

A hybrid of *C. epigejos* and *C. arundinacea* that grows naturally but sparsely in Europe, and rarely produces viable seed. It and both parent species are upright, cool-season growers. For years plants representing this cross were known as *C. epigejos* 'Hortorum', then *C. ×acutiflora* 'Stricta', and now 'Karl Foerster'. Side-by-side trials in Longwood Gardens have proved plants sold as 'Stricta' and 'Karl Foerster' to be identical. In the future, if other clonal selections are made with similar hybrid origin, they cannot be called 'Stricta'.

'Karl Foerster' ('Stricta'). Karl Foerster feather reed grass. One of the most popular ornamental grasses worldwide. It is beautiful, versatile, and needs almost no care. The deep green, lustrous foliage is effective by early spring and lasts into winter. Clump-forming and strictly upright, it produces vertical inflorescences to 6 ft. (2 m) that are loosely feathered and subtly purplish when they first appear in early summer. By late summer they become narrow vertical plumes of a delicate buff color, remaining upright and attractive through most of winter. Suitable for fresh or dry arrangements. This limber grass is one of the best for introducing motion to the garden; it moves gracefully with even a barely perceptible breeze.

In late July, *Calamagrostis ×acutiflora* 'Karl Foerster' adds vertical accents to a North Carolina landscape.

Drying plumes of *Calamagrostis* ×*acutiflora* 'Karl Foerster' flicker like candles when a late June breeze moves them in and out of the path of summer sunrays.

Calamagrostis ×*acutiflora* 'Overdam' in mid-July in England.

Always regains its upright posture even after heavy rains and never needs staking. Stunning as a specimen or vertical accent. An excellent screen due to fast growth, reliability, and multiseason duration. Can be used for large-scale residential or commercial plantings without fear of compromising adjacent natural areas. Tolerates full sun to half shade. Grows best on well-drained fertile soils with adequate moisture, but tolerates heavy clays. May suffer from disfiguring foliar rust diseases in wet summers, especially if air circulation is poor. Cut back to about 5 in. (12 cm) by early March. Divide or transplant in spring or fall. Plants in containers make attractive specimens and survive most winters without protection. Zone 4.

'Overdam'. Variegated feather reed grass. Similar to 'Karl Foerster' except the foliage is striped longitudinally with cream-white, and plants and flowers are less robust. Variegation is most pronounced in climates with low humidity and cool summer nights. Suffers in hot, humid weather. Zone 5.

Calamagrostis brachytricha is tinted red-purple when first flowering in mid-September in Maryland.

A sweep of *Calamagrostis brachytricha* is strong and upright in full sun in late September in Illinois.

Calamagrostis brachytricha
Korean feather reed grass

A variable species from eastern Asia, where it most frequently grows in moist woodlands and at the edges of woods. Introduced to Western gardens from seed collected from plants growing wild in Korea. More of a warm-season grower, flowering in September. The inflorescences begin with a strong purple-red tint, fading to silver-gray, remaining open and feathery even when dry, unlike C. ×acutiflora 'Karl Foerster'. Flowers last into winter, suitable for fresh or dry arrangements. Clump-forming, upright-arching in overall form, to 4 ft. (1.2 m) tall in flower. Sometimes attractively lax in growth. Foliage slightly coarse in appearance, with glossy green leaves to ½ in. (12 mm) wide. Fall foliage an undistinguished yellow. Easily grown on a range of soils in partial shade or in full sun if provided with sufficient moisture. Self-sows in moist shady situations but is easily managed. Cut back by late winter. Propagate by seed or by division in spring. Effective as a specimen, in groups or masses. An excellent container subject. Zone 4.

Calamagrostis canadensis
Bluejoint

Native to marshes, wet places, open woods, and meadows across much of northern North America. Of minor ornamental importance. Not as fluffy in flower as the Eurasian species and not as well behaved as the clump-forming western U.S.

Arching flower clusters of *Calamagrostis foliosa* are green with noticeably yellow anthers in mid-May in California.

The drying plumes of *Calamagrostis foliosa* are attractively tawny in mid-August in California.

species. Runs strongly by rhizomes and self-sows prolifically. Foliage sometimes tinted burgundy in autumn. Zone 3.

Calamagrostis foliosa
Leafy reed grass, Mendocino reed grass

A highly ornamental species native to coastal bluffs, cliffs, scrub, and forest in northern California. Tufted and clump-forming, to 2 ft. (60 cm) tall. Blooms May to August, producing arching sprays of feathery flowers above the blue-green foliage. Ideal for sloping sites, forming a floral cascade. In California, prefers light shade, moderate moisture, and good drainage. Foliage semi-evergreen. Propagate by seed or division. Zone 8, possibly colder.

Calamagrostis nutkaensis
Pacific reed grass

Native along the Pacific Coast in moist soil or wet forested hills from Alaska to central California. Tufted and clump-forming to 3–5 ft. (1–1.5 m) tall. Foliage rather coarse, semi-evergreen in mild

climates. Feathery inflorescences open purplish in spring, drying to a straw color. Does well in full sun if soil is moist. Somewhat salt tolerant. A cool-season grower, it may suffer from foliar rusts in overly wet or humid midsummer periods. Propagate by seed or division. Zone 7.

Calamagrostis ophitidus
Serpentine reed grass

Grows on serpentine soils in northern California. Tufted and strictly clump-forming to 3 ft. (1 m) tall. Upright in form, resembling C. ×acutiflora 'Karl Foerster' but more delicate and better adapted to infertile soils in a warm climate. Propagate by seed. Zone 8.

CAREX
Sedge (Sedge family)

In the broad sense, the word *sedge* refers to any of the nearly 3600 species that make up the sedge family, but in the more usual, narrower sense, the word refers to any of nearly 1000 species comprising the huge genus *Carex*. Most

Calamagrostis nutkaensis flowering in mid-June in California.

Calamagrostis ophitidus in mid-August in California.

Carex albula in early August.

Carex baccans in early February in California.

ornamental sedge species originate from moist or wet habitats in temperate regions around the world. They are too little known and too little used in the garden. Flowers are often of minor ornamental importance, but foliage colors match or exceed the diversity found in grasses. In the garden sedges can be specimens, accents, groundcovers, lawns, or container specimens. Most can be propagated by division in late spring. Deciduous sedges should be cut back annually in spring. Evergreen or semi-evergreen sedges are best cut back occasionally as necessary in late spring to remove old or winter-desiccated foliage.

Carex albula
Blonde sedge, frosted curls sedge

One of the best and most distinctive New Zealand natives, producing cascading fountains of the finest-textured foliage. So light green it appears silver from a short distance. Best planted on slopes, in pots, or other places where its foliage can trail. Flowers insignificant. Prefers sun to part shade. Tolerates various soils and drought. Often confused with *C. comans*, or sold as a cultivar, variously named "Frosted Curls" or "Frosty Curls," but these are common names. This is a distinct species that is uniform when grown from seed. Self-sows to a pleasant extent in milder climates. Zone 7, possibly colder.

Carex baccans
Crimson-seeded sedge

Native to India, Sri Lanka, and China. An unusual sedge, valued primarily for the bright red of the inflorescences as seeds ripen. A coarse-textured plant, with medium-green leaves ½ in. (12 mm) wide, flowering stems to 3 ft. (1 m) tall. Flowers are green in summer, turn red by late autumn, and remain colorful during winter in mild climates. Best in partial shade, fertile soil, with plenty of moisture. Good near streamsides. Propagate by seed or by division in spring. Zone 8.

Carex buchananii
Leatherleaf sedge

One of the best known and most popular New Zealand natives. Tufted and erect in growth, especially when young. The narrow foliage is copper-bronze, to 2 ft. (60 cm) tall, and best in full sun. The bronze-leaved New Zealand sedges can be stunning if contrasted with silvers or with flower colors. When viewed against bare soil or

Carex buchananii with violets in late May in New York.

mulch, they look dead. Needs good drainage for hardiness in colder zones. Propagate by seed or by division in spring. Zone 7.

Carex caryophyllea
Spring sedge
Native to Europe. In England, grows in calcareous grasslands and on acid mountain soils. Leaves dark green, recurving, to 12 in. (30 cm). Ornamentally important only for the following cultivar.

'The Beatles'. May be a hybrid, but is believed by many to belong in this species. Makes a deep green mop of narrow foliage 6 in. (15 cm) tall, spreading slowly. A useful low groundcover, evergreen in milder climates. Requires moisture. Zone 5.

Carex comans
New Zealand hairy sedge
This New Zealand native was one of the earliest to reach Western gardens. It is quite distinct from *C. buchananii* in form, with pendent, flowing

Carex comans in mid-July in England.

Carex conica
'Snowline' in
mid-July in
England.

Carex
dolichostachya
'Kaga Nishiki' in
mid-September in
Delaware.

foliage. Typically bronze-colored, best in full sun with good drainage. Many New Zealand sedges exhibit leaf color variations from green to bronze, and this has caused much confusion. Many green-leaved plants offered commercially as *C. comans* var. *stricta* and most offered as 'Frosted Curls' or 'Frosty Curls' are *C. albula*. Zone 7.

'Bronze'. Foliage deeply bronze-colored all year. Zone 7.

Carex conica
Hime kan suge
Suge is the Japanese name for sedge. Common in open woods on hillsides and low mountains in Japan, also native to southern Korea. Densely tufted, forming a neat mound of narrow, glossy green foliage. Leaves $3/16$ in. (4 mm) wide. Known ornamentally for the following variegated cultivar.

'Snowline' ('Marginata', 'Variegata'). Leaves deep green with conspicuous white edges. Long-lived but slow to increase in size, which has led to the belief that there are different-sized cultivars. Eventually, with good soil and adequate moisture, this plant can grow to 15 in. (38 cm) tall by 24 in. (60 cm) wide. Best in light shade in climates with intense summer sun. Evergreen in mild climates. In colder climates, cut foliage back if winter damaged, just before new growth begins in spring. Zone 5.

Carex crinita flowering in native habitat in northern Delaware in mid-June.

Foliage of variegated sedges (from top): *Carex conica* 'Snowline', *C. elata* 'Aurea', *C. dolichostachya* 'Kaga Nishiki', *C. morrowii* var. *temnolepis* 'Silk Tassel', *C. morrowii* 'Ice Dance', *C. oshimensis* 'Evergold' (older foliage), *C. oshimensis* 'Evergold' (new foliage).

Carex crinita
Fringed sedge

Native to wet woods and swales in eastern North America. Similar in appearance to the European native *C. pendula* but much more cold hardy. A large species, to 4 ft. (1.2 m) tall to the top of the arching inflorescences, which are produced in early summer and last into late autumn. Architecturally interesting. Pliant stems move gracefully with woodland breezes. Largest in a moist or wet shady site, but can be grown on soils of average moisture in part sun. Propagate by seed or by division in spring. Zone 5.

Carex dolichostachya
Miyama kan suge

Native to Japanese mountain woodlands. Important ornamentally for the following variegated cultivar.

'Kaga Nishiki' ('Gold Fountains'). Kaga brocade sedge. In Japanese, *Kaga* is the old name for the Ishikawa Prefecture and *nishiki* means

"brocade," an apt description for the lacy beauty of this finely gold-variegated sedge. A superb selection, leaves to 3/16 in. (4 mm) wide, medium green in center and gold at the edges, forming a symmetrical fountainlike mound, eventually to 2 ft. (60 cm) in diameter. Long-lived and durable. Suited for accent or groundcover sweeps. Light shade or full sun with adequate moisture. Prefers fertile organic soils. Reasonably drought tolerant. Propagate by division in spring. Zone 5, evergreen into zone 6.

Carex elata
Tufted sedge, European tussock-sedge

Native to swamps, mires, fens, edges of lakes, and riverbanks in northern and eastern Europe. Forms dense tussocks, sometimes in extensive stands. Analogous in form and preferred habitat to the North American *C. stricta*. The green-

Carex elata 'Aurea' flowering in mid-May in Washington State.

Carex elata 'Aurea' in shallow water in Pennsylvania in early June.

leaved species is not often cultivated, but the variegated forms are perhaps the most brightly colored of all sedges.

'Aurea' ('Bowles Golden'). Bowles' golden sedge. Graham Stuart Thomas quoted E. A. Bowles's description of this as "a very beautiful sedge, with golden-striped leaves, another of my finds in the Norfolk Broads." This graceful plant grows upright to 2½ ft. (80 cm). The leaves are up to ⁵⁄₁₆ in. (8 mm) wide, mostly yellow with faint, random longitudinal green stripes. Yellow color is most intense when grown in full sun. Foliage looks good through the growing season on plants at waterside or even shallowly submerged. Burns if too dry, losing much appeal by late summer. Shady site is necessary in drier soils, in which case leaves are rich lime-yellow in color. Does not do well in hot climates. Vertical inflorescences in early May are subtly attractive, soon disappearing amid developing foliage. Propagate by division in spring. Zone 5.

'Knightshayes'. Similar to 'Aurea' but leaves yellow.

Carex flacca
Glaucous sedge, carnation grass

Native to calcareous grasslands, sand dunes, and estuary marshes in Europe. Also native to northern Africa and naturalized in eastern North America. A variable species growing 6–24 in. (15–60 cm) tall, with leaves to ³⁄₁₆ in. (4 mm) wide, sometimes green above and glaucous-blue below, sometimes glaucous-blue on both sides, resulting in an attractive bluish overall appearance. The foliage is similar in color to that of carnation leaves, hence the common name. Many different forms are in cultivation, some intensely blue and short, others greener or taller. Dry conditions limit height. Flowers, appearing in late spring on culms to 12 in. (30 cm) tall, are relatively insignificant even though purple-black in color. Strongly rhizomatous, this species spreads slowly but steadily to form dense, fine-textured masses and is very useful as a groundcover in full sun to light shade. Very drought tolerant. Adaptable to a wide range of soils, including alkaline types, and can also withstand some salinity. Most plants sold in the United States as *C. nigra* are actually *C. flacca*. The individual flowers of *C. flacca* have three stigmas; flowers of *C. nigra* have two stigmas. Zone 4.

'Bias'. Leaves variegated on one side.

Carex flacca in late May.

Carex flaccosperma var. *glaucodea* in the author's Pennsylvania garden in late November.

Carex flagellifera in mid-August in Washington State.

Carex grayi in early June in eastern Pennsylvania.

Carex montana in mid-July in England.

Carex lupulina in moist woodlands in northern Delaware in mid-June.

Carex flaccosperma

Native to rich, often calcareous woods and bottomlands in eastern North America, forming loose tussocks of green to glaucous blue-green leaves, ⅝ in. (15 mm) wide. The basal leaves last through winter, so this sedge is essentially evergreen. Relatively insignificant flowers appear in early spring. Fairly drought tolerant. Not particular about soil. Propagate by seed or by division in spring. Zone 5.

Carex flaccosperma var. glaucodea

Bluer than the typical species and a subtly attractive addition to shady or partly shady gardens.

Carex flagellifera

A New Zealand native very similar to *C. buchananii* but less vertical, even when young, and scarcely distinguishable from bronze plants of *C. comans*. Zone 7.

Carex grayi
Gray's sedge, mace sedge

Named for eminent American botanist Asa Gray (1810–1888). A clump-forming native of eastern North American meadows and alluvial woodlands. To 3 ft. (1 m) tall, leafy, medium-green. Flowering in May, producing conspicuous and attractive light green seed-heads, shaped like maces, ¾–1½ in. (2–4 cm) diameter at maturity. Shade to part sun. Needs moisture. Propagate by seed or by division in spring. Zone 5b.

'**Morning Star**'. A selection with seed-heads 1 in. (25 mm) wide.

Carex hachijoensis
Hachijo kan suge

Native to Hachijo Island off Japan's main island, Honshu. Not as cold hardy as the similar but more densely tufted *C. oshimensis*, and probably not in cultivation in Western gardens. The variegated cultivar 'Evergold' belongs to *C. oshimensis*.

Carex lupulina
Hop sedge

Native to wet woods and swamps from Nova Scotia to Minnesota south to Florida and Texas. Deciduous, clump-forming, with upright stems to 30 in. (75 cm) tall and medium green leaves to ½ in. (12 mm) wide. Flowers abundantly in late spring to early summer. The dramatic female spikes are to 1¼ in. (32 mm) long and hoplike in appearance. Larger-flowered but lesser known than Gray's sedge, *C. grayi*, this species is worth trying in moist or wet woodland gardens. Adapted to periodic standing water. Sunny dry sites cause yellowing of growth. Propagates readily by seed or division. Zone 4.

Carex montana
Mountain sedge

Native from eastern Europe to central Asia. A narrow-leaved rhizomatous species useful as a groundcover, usually growing less than 2 ft. (60 cm) tall. Evergreen or semi-evergreen even in colder climates. Tolerates alkaline soils. Propagate by division in spring or by seed. Zone 4.

Carex morrowii 'Gilt' in early July in Pennsylvania.

Carex morrowii var. *morrowii*
Kan suge

Native to woods in low mountains of central and southern Japan. The leaves are typically solid green, but variegated forms were introduced to Western horticulture by the mid-1800s. Among gardeners and the nursery industry, *C. morrowii* often serves as a catch-all name for Japanese sedges, resulting in much confusion. In cultivation, it is correctly represented by two distinct varieties, one of which is var. *morrowii* with thick, leathery leaves to ½ in. (12 mm) wide and somewhat coarse textured. Generally clump-forming or slowly rhizomatous, evergreen except in the coldest climates. Very long-lived plants of easy culture on a wide range of soils. The rhizomatous forms are especially suited for groundcover use. Zone 5.

'**Gilt**'. Distinct cream-white leaf margins. Introduced from Japan. Slowly rhizomatous.

'**Gold Band**'. Slightly wider, cream-yellow variegated leaf margins than typical for plants sold as 'Variegata'.

Carex morrowii 'Silver Sceptre' in the author's Pennsylvania garden in mid-July.

'Ice Dance'. Strong cream-white marginal variegation. Rhizomatous and carpet-forming. Knits together but not invasive. Introduced from Japan.

'Silver Sceptre'. A dramatic variegated form from the garden of Masato Yokoi in Japan. The leaves, up to 5/16 in. (9 mm) wide, have broad cream-white margins and green midsections. The foliage is softer and less leathery than typical for *C. morrowii*, and further investigation may prove this to belong to a related species. Foliage to 12 in. (30 cm) tall. Zone 6, probably zone 5.

'Variegata'. Not a clonal cultivar, but a name suitable for any of the numerous, otherwise unnamed selections of the species having white leaf margins in common. The variegated margins may be distinct or barely conspicuous.

Carex morrowii var. temnolepis
Hosoba kan suge

Native to mountain woods on Japan's main island, Honshu. Having threadlike leaves just over 1/8 in. (3 mm) wide, this botanical variety is so different from the typical variety that it is difficult for casual observers to believe it represents the same species. In fact, nineteenth-century botanist Adrien Franchet originally thought it to be a distinct species.

'Silk Tassel'. Leaves only 1/8 in. (3 mm) wide, dark green at margins and clear white at center, forming an exquisite fountain of shimmering, fine-textured foliage. Eventually to 1 ft. (30 cm) tall by 2 ft. (60 cm) wide. Grow in sun with moisture or in shade. Introduced from Japan. Zone 5.

Carex muskingumensis
Palm sedge

Native to low woods and wet meadows in north-central North America. Creeping by rhizomes. Numerous narrow, tapered leaves radiate from lax stems growing to 2 ft. (60 cm) tall. Capable of forming large groundcover masses. Flowering in early June, neither adding nor detracting significantly from appearance. Grow in full sun and moist soil or in shade. Propagate by division in spring. Typical leaves colored a solid medium-green. Zone 4.

Carex morrowii var. *temnolepis* 'Silk Tassel' in mid-July in North Carolina.

Carex muskingumensis
in early October in
Maryland.

Carex muskingumensis
'Little Midge' in mid-July
in Pennsylvania.

Carex muskingumensis
'Oehme' yellow-
margined leaves.

Carex muskingumensis 'Ice Fountain' in May in an Oregon greenhouse.

'Ice Fountain'. Boldly variegated. The leaves are green at margins with cream-white in the middle. Not as cold hardy as the green-leafed typical form.

'Little Midge'. Smaller in all aspects, typically less than 1 ft. (30 cm) tall.

'Oehme'. Leaves with thin yellow margins in spring, becoming evenly green as the season progresses. A sport from Wolfgang Oehme's garden. Zone 4.

'Silberstreif'. Leaves green and white variegated, slightly smaller-growing.

'Wachtposten' ('Sentry Tower'). Typical of the species, perhaps with slightly more erect stems.

Carex nigra
Black-flowering sedge

This extremely variable species is native to bogs, marshes, and streamsides in Europe and to eastern coastal North America. Grows 1–2½ ft. (30–80 cm) tall, spreading by rhizomes or (particularly in American native forms) forming dense tussocks. Leaves often glaucous-blue, to ³⁄₁₆ in. (4 mm) wide. Flowers in late spring, the female flowers blackish, interesting but not showy. Most plants sold by this name in the United States are correctly *C. flacca*. The individual flowers of *C. flacca* have three stigmas; flowers of *C. nigra* have two stigmas. Zone 5.

'Variegata'. Leaves glaucous-green with thin marginal light yellow variegation. To 12 in. (30 cm) tall, spreading. Small blackish flowers in late spring; two stigmas. Full sun or light shade. Zone 5.

Carex nudata
California black-flowering sedge

Native along wet sandy or rocky streambeds, below the high-water mark, in northern California. Densely tufted, forming raised tussocks reminiscent of the eastern North American *C. stricta*. Flowers truly black when opening in late winter or early spring, conspicuous, and ornamental, held on arching stems above the foliage, to 2 ft. (60 cm). Best in sun with moisture. An interesting

Carex nudata flowering in March in a Pennsylvania greenhouse.

container specimen for colder climates. Propagate by seed or by division in spring. Zone 7.

Carex ornithopoda
Bird's-foot sedge

Native to Europe. Tufted narrow green leaves, low growing. The variegated selection is most frequently grown. Zone 7.

'Variegata'. Leaves striped white. Diminutive, to 8 in. (20 cm) tall, slow growing, well suited to rock gardens. Sometimes confused in the nursery trade with young plants of *C. oshimensis* 'Evergold'.

Carex oshimensis
Oshima kan suge

Native and common in dry woods and rocky slopes throughout Honshu Island, Japan. Represented in cultivation mostly by the variegated forms.

'Evergold' ('Aureo-variegata', 'Everbrite', 'Old Gold', 'Variegata'). One of the most ornamental and widely grown variegated sedges. Densely tufted, forming a thick, spilling tussock of fine-tex-

tured foliage to 16 in. (40 cm) tall. Leaves glossy to $5/16$ in. (8 mm) wide, dark green at the margins, with a broad median stripe that is cream-white on emerging foliage, maturing to cream-yellow. Flowers are ornamentally insignificant. This cultivar is often listed as belonging to *C. hachijoensis*, a species that is similar but is less tufted, has slightly wider leaves, flowers later, and is less hardy. Performs well in a broad range of cultural conditions but suffers in extreme heat. A truly beautiful sedge, useful as accent, in groups, groundcover masses, or as a container subject. Zone 6.

'Gold Strike'. Uniform, richly cream-yellow median stripes. Zone 6.

Carex pansa
California meadow sedge

Native to coastal sands in California and Washington. John Greenlee of California pioneered the use of this species as an alternative to typical turf-grass lawns. Rich green foliage is somewhat tousled, to 6 in. (15 cm) tall if unmowed. Spreads

Carex oshimensis 'Gold Strike' in late September in the author's Pennsylvania garden.

Carex pansa in early February in California.

Carex pendula ornaments an English courtyard in early July.

sufficiently by rhizomes to form a solid carpet, but not invasive. Dormant in summer unless watered in warmer, drier regions. Full sun to medium shade. Best established by planting plugs. Zone 8.

Carex pendula
Great drooping sedge, pendulous sedge

A wide-ranging species, native to Europe, Asia, and northern Africa. Clump-forming, with gracefully arching stems to 6 ft. (2 m) tall, from which hang delicate, cylindrical male and female flower spikes. It self-sows freely and is the quintessential, accidental tourist in British gardens. Although most texts suggest relegating it to the wilder parts of the garden, it is sometimes the perfect architectural counterpoint to a stone wall or spare courtyard of a stately home, where it will be content to grow between cracks in the pavers. Zone 8.

'Moonraker'. A strikingly cream-yellow variegated cultivar pulled out of a hedgerow in Wiltshire, England, by a farmer's tractor. The variega-

tion is most pronounced in the early, cooler part of the growing season. Propagates slowly by division. Zone 8.

Carex pensylvanica
Pennsylvania sedge

Native to thickets and woods in eastern North America. Individual plants of this apparently delicate little sedge are so slight they are easy to overlook; however, this durable species is highly suited for use as a lawn alternative, planted thickly in dry sunny or shady sites. It is capable of producing a soft, uniform cover of green even in dry, sandy, wooded settings. Semi-evergreen in mild to moderately cold climates. It has proved useful as a mowable groundcover in lightly shaded parking lot islands at the Chicago Botanic Garden. Slender green leaves grow to 8 in. (20 cm) tall or can be mowed as low as 2 in. (5 cm). May flowers are insignificant. Propagate by seed or by division in spring. Zone 4.

'Hilltop'. A low-growing selection from Maryland.

Carex pensylvanica forms a natural groundcover under beeches in mid-July in the mountains of North Carolina.

Carex pensylvanica
foliage is very
fine textured
and grasslike.

Carex
phyllocephala
'Sparkler' in late
September in
Pennsylvania.

Carex phyllocephala
Tenjiku suge

An unusual Chinese native, originally introduced to Japan for medicinal use. Leaves nearly in whorls, clustered toward the top of the 2-ft. (60-cm) tall canelike stems. The green-leaved plant is interesting, but not showy. Sometimes surviving zone 6 winters, it is more cold hardy than the spectacular variegated sport, which originated in Japan. Best in fertile organic soil with adequate moisture.

Propagate by seed or division. Self-sows manageably. Zone 7.

'Sparkler'. Fuiri tenjiku suge. *Fuiri* means "variegated" in Japanese. This stunningly variegated selection was introduced from Japan. The leaves are dark green in the center with broad, conspicuous white to cream-white margins, creating an overall white effect. Makes an excellent summer container specimen in zones too cold for permanent planting in-ground. Grows well in part shade, or in full sun with plenty of moisture. Zone 8.

Carex plantaginea
in late July in
North Carolina.

Carex platyphylla
in mid-July in
Pennsylvania.

Carex plantaginea
Plantain-leafed sedge,
broad-leafed sedge

Native to rich moist woods in eastern North America. Clump-forming. Leaves unusually broad, to 1⅛ in. (3 cm) wide, shiny green, with prominent parallel veins. The basal leaves overwinter, so the plant is effectively evergreen. A delightful bold-textured companion to ferns and woodland wildflowers in native habitats and in the garden. Requires regular moisture and part shade for best growth. Propagate by seed or by division in spring. Zone 5.

Carex platyphylla
Broad-leafed sedge, silver sedge

Grows natively on rocky slopes and streambanks in rich deciduous woodlands from Maine and southern Quebec south to the North Carolina mountains and west to Wisconsin and Missouri. Perhaps the most dramatic of the glaucous-leafed North American native sedges. Leaves

¾–1 in. (20–25 mm) wide and usually strongly glaucous, sometimes nearly silver in appearance. Forms a loose, low tuft of leaves, usually less than 5 in. (13 cm) in height. Produces new leaves in spring that remain attractive through most or all of winter. The spring flowering stalks are spare and horticulturally insignificant. Will tolerate calcareous soils. Prefers moist organic soil. Grows well in deep deciduous shade or in partly sunny sites. Can be grown underneath deciduous shrubs. Propagates readily by seed or division in spring. Zone 4.

Carex riparia
Greater pond sedge
Widespread throughout the Northern Hemisphere, often forming large stands around ponds, by slow-moving rivers, and by other wet places. Spreads aggressively by rhizomes. Typically green-leaved, stems to 4 ft. (1.2 m) tall.

'**Variegata**'. Variegated pond sedge. Long arching leaves are boldly striped white. Occasional all-white leaves are produced in spring. Full sun, moist or wet. Can be an invasive runner. Zone 6.

Carex riparia 'Variegata' in England in mid-July.

Carex siderosticha
Creeping broad-leafed sedge, tagane-so
Native to mountain woods in Japan, Korea, Manchuria, and China. Slowly creeping by rhizomes, forming a dense mass of bold-textured foliage. Leaves 1¼ in. (32 mm) wide, solid green, to 8 in. (20 cm) tall. Prefers part shade, moisture, fertile soil. This is a long-lived, durable sedge for woodland gardens. The typical green-leaved form is rarely offered commercially, although it is a fine garden plant. The variegated cultivars are most commonly encountered. Zone 5.

'**Banana Boat**'. Dan Heims of Terra Nova Nurseries in Oregon made this striking yellow variegated form from Japan available commercially.

'**Island Brocade**'. Another recent variegated selection introduced from Japan. Leaves are approximately 1 in. (30 cm) wide and usually less than 5 in. (13 cm) long, green at center with bold cream-yellow margins. Stems somewhat more

trailing than *C. siderosticha* 'Variegata'. Makes a superb container specimen. Zone 5.

'**Variegata**'. Striped broad-leafed sedge. Leaves green with clear white stripes, especially toward the margins. One of the most strikingly ornamental hardy sedges. Provided moisture and partial shade, it is beautiful from the time the new spring foliage emerges until autumn. The new leaves are sometimes attractively tinted pink during cool springs. Fully deciduous in winter. To 8 in. (20 cm) tall. Spreads slowly by rhizomes. Propagates easily by division in spring. Superb for accent or in groundcover patches to brighten a woodland garden. Zone 6.

Carex spissa
San Diego sedge
Native along watercourses in southern California. Striking gray-blue leaves to 5 ft. (1.5 m) tall distinguish this sedge from all others. Spreads slowly by rhizomes, forming large clumps but never invasive. Quite beautiful when planted at

Carex siderosticha
'Banana Boat' in
Pennsylvania in
mid-August.

Carex siderosticha 'Island
Brocade' in a hanging
basket in May in Oregon.

Carex siderosticha
'Variegata' in mid-June
in Pennsylvania.

Carex spissa in mid-December in California.

Carex stricta flowers in early May in its native habitat in eastern Pennsylvania.

water's edge. Dark black-brown inflorescences to 18 in. (45 cm) in spring. Foliage is evergreen, but is best cut back occasionally, as necessary, to remove accumulations of dead or discolored leaves. Does well in southeastern United States if grown in water or moist soil, but self-sows. Cut back after flowering to avoid unwanted seedlings. Propagate by seed or division. Zone 7.

Carex stricta
Tussock sedge

Native to wet swales, marshes, and creeksides in northeastern North America. Similar in form and preferred habitat to the European *C. elata*. Develops dense tussocks raised above water's surface, each with an accumulation of old leaves surrounding the base. Spreads by underground rhizomes to form new tussocks, sometimes creating large stands. Rich green and fine-textured, beautiful in contrast to skunk cabbage (*Symplo-*

carpus foetidus), cinnamon fern (*Osmunda cinnamomea*), and other eastern natives of wet woods and the edges of woods. Can be grown away from water if soil is moist. Zone 4.

Carex testacea
Orange New Zealand sedge

A common native on New Zealand's North and South Islands. Clump-forming, making a fine-textured mound of foliage to 15 in. (38 cm) tall, copper-brown in summer with distinct orange tints in winter. Appreciates moisture, good drainage. Self-sows pleasantly. One of the more cold hardy New Zealand sedges. Zone 6.

Carex tumulicola
Berkeley sedge, foot-hill sedge

Native on dry soil from Washington south through Oregon and in coastal California south to Monterey. Creeping by rhizomes, foliage deep green, to 18 in.

Carex testacea in England in mid-July.

Carex tumulicola in California in early February.

(45 cm) tall, fully evergreen in milder climates. When planted densely, creates a lush groundcover. Can be mowed periodically to create a more turflike effect. Drought tolerant, water conserving. Propagate by seed or by division in spring. Zone 7.

CHASMANTHIUM
Wild-oats, wood-oats (Grass family)

Comprised of six species native to eastern North America and northern Mexico. Only *C. latifolium* is commonly grown ornamentally. It is closely related to and was once included in the genus *Uniola*, sea-oats, although *C. latifolium* is an inland species, and any appellation referring to the sea is a misnomer.

Chasmanthium latifolium
Indian wood-oats, river-oats

Native to wooded slopes, moist thickets, and river bottoms from Texas north to Pennsylvania and New Jersey. A clump-forming, warm-season grower to 4 ft. (1.2 m) in rich moist soil. Very upright in sun, attractively lax-stemmed in shade. In intensely sunny regions, needs moisture for good green foliage color in sun. Grows well even in very dry shade. In England it requires full sun. Especially valued for the dangling oatlike spikelets, held on slender nodding stems above the foliage. Begins flowering in midsummer. Spikelets light green at first, becoming red-bronze in autumn and finally light salmon-buff, remaining attractive

Chasmanthium latifolium in part shade in early August in Maryland.

Chasmanthium latifolium in sun in Pennsylvania, turning tawny in early October.

The setting rays of the autumn sun light up the foliage and seed-heads of *Chasmanthium latifolium* in the author's former Delaware garden.

through winter, especially encased in ice or dusted with snow. Worth growing just for fresh cut or dried arrangements. Leaves to ¾ in. (2 cm) wide and to 8 in. (20 cm) long, medium green in summer, turning a vibrant gold in autumn. Of easy culture on a wide range of soils. Self-sows readily in moist gardens, but seedlings are easily scratched out when young. Cut back in spring before new growth begins. A versatile grass for formal accent, groups, sweeps, groundcover, naturalizing, or container display. Propagate by seed or by division in spring. Zone 5.

CHIONOCHLOA
Snow grass, tussock grass (Grass family)
Comprised of approximately 20 species native to New Zealand and Australia, mostly in alpine and subalpine zones, all clumping and forming dense tussocks. Some valued for flowers, many for foliage texture. Closely related to *Danthonia* and *Cortaderia*. Propagate by seed or division.

Chionochloa flavicans
Green-leaved tussock grass
Native to high elevations in New Zealand. Similar to *C. flavescens* but leaves green. Needs strong sun for flowering, but best in regions with cool nights. Summer blooming. Useful for cut or dried flowers. Zone 8.

Chionochloa rubra
Red tussock grass
Widespread and sometimes growing in great drifts in lowland and low-alpine areas in the volcanic mountains of New Zealand. Common on the mineral belts of the South Island and on poorly drained peaty valley floors or rolling slopes mostly below the tree line. Not especially showy in flower, but attractive for the strong red-copper foliage. Shorter than *C. flavicans* when in flower. Zone 8.

CHONDROPETALUM
Restio family
Comprised of approximately 15 rushlike, dioecious species native to the South African Cape

region, forming tussocks to 6 ft. (2 m). They are part of the fynbos plant community, which is characterized by frequently occurring natural fires, and are generally found on well-drained soils low in fertility. Cool-season growers, they are most active in spring and autumn but have an evergreen presence. Many are quite beautiful but little known in cultivation. They are suitable for gardens in Mediterranean and warm temperate regions.

Chondropetalum tectorum
Grows in South African marshes and seeps. Forms an erect tussock to 4 ft. (1.2) tall, very slowly rhizomatous. Stems rich dark green,

Chionochloa flavicans in California in mid-June.

Chionochloa rubra in native habitat on New Zealand's South Island in early October.

Chondropetalum tectorum in mid-September in South Africa.

unbranched, and bare of recognizable leaves, giving the appearance of a huge common rush, *Juncus effusus*, but more relaxed, the stems radiating in an arc and touching the ground. Male and female flowers on separate plants, similar in appearance, dark brown, narrowly clustered at the tips of stems. A beautifully sculptural plant, stunning when moving in the wind or catching sunrays. Propagate by seed. Difficult to divide as the roots do not like to be disturbed. Does not do well in highly fertile soils. Best planted in spring or autumn in Mediterranean climates. An excellent seasonal container subject in areas beyond its winter cold hardiness. Zone 8.

CORTADERIA
Pampas grass, tussock grass
(Grass family)

Comprised of approximately 25 species of large, tussock-forming grasses, mostly native to South America but also to New Zealand and New Guinea, usually in open habitats. Closely related to *Chionochloa*. Appreciated ornamentally for their grand size and huge flower plumes. In mild regions, pampas grasses are undemanding and long-lived if provided a sunny site, fertile soil, and adequate moisture. The tussocks are best cut back occasionally, with gloved hands and pruners or power shears. Although a few of the smaller selections are cold hardy in zone 6, most *Cortaderia* species require more warmth. Plants promoted in colder zones as "hardy pampas grass" are sometimes, in fact, *Saccharum ravennae*, which is best called ravenna grass. Propagate by division in spring.

Cortaderia richardii
Plumed tussock, tussock grass

Native to moist, open places in New Zealand. Although the plumes are not as large and full, this species truly rivals the majesty of pampas grass, *C. selloana*. It grows to 10 ft. (3 m) tall in bloom, with the inflorescences often gently nodding on top of a multitude of stalks ascending at different angles from the center of the clump. Plumes nearly white or with a slight, attractive brassy tint, often slightly one-sided. Blooms mid to late summer. A magnificent grass for streamside or pond-

Cortaderia richardii in mid-July in England.

side. Needs moisture, not as drought tolerant or as cold hardy as the Argentine species. Zone 8.

Cortaderia selloana
Pampas grass

Native to Brazil, Argentina, and Chile. The quintessential ornamental grass of the Victorian era. Outstanding for fresh or dried floral bouquets. Mature plants can top 10 ft. (3 m) in height, with nearly equal spread. The flower stalks are held erect, produced in late summer and early autumn, and remain attractive into winter. The foliage is evergreen in mild climates, green or often strikingly gray-green. Accustomed to moist winters and hot summers in its native habitat, this warm-season grower is well adapted to gardens in the southeastern United States, where it has become a beautiful cliché. Requires full sun but tolerates varying soils, and established plants are extremely drought tolerant. Propagate, divide, or transplant only in late spring or early summer. Best in large gardens. The foliage of variegated cultivars is so striking that these are worth growing in containers in cold areas, or they may be planted in the ground each season and dug and overwintered in a cold frame. Such treatment dramatically reduces the plant's size and often results in a lack of flowering. Zone 8.

'Albolineata' ('Silver Stripe'). White-striped pampas grass. A long-established selection with leaves longitudinally striped white. Valued primarily for the variegated foliage, which is most distinct later in season. Plumes white, modest-sized. Zone 8.

'Andes Silver'. Plumes silver, 7 ft. (2.1 m). More cold hardy than the species. Zone 6.

'Aureolineata' ('Gold Band'). Golden-variegated pampas grass. Leaves with dramatic longitudinal yellow stripes mostly near the margins, but some blades nearly all-yellow. Valued primarily for the foliage, which is most intensely colored later in season. Plumes white, modest-sized. An excellent container subject. Zone 8.

'Bertini'. Compact-growing, to only 3 ft. (1 m) in flower. Plumes white.

'Monvin'. Yellow-striped leaves. Introduced and patented by Monrovia Nursery of California, and marketed under the name Sun Stripe™.

Cortaderia selloana in Wisconsin in mid-June.

Cortaderia selloana 'Aureolineata' catches the mid-October sun in southern California.

Morning sun illuminates the flowing foliage of *Cortaderia selloana* 'Aureolineata' in mid-June in southern California.

'Patagonia'. Plumes silver, to 6 ft. (2 m). Leaves bluish gray-green. More cold hardy than the species. Zone 6.

'Pink Feather'. Plumes large, with pink blush. Zone 8.

'Pumila'. Compact pampas grass. Plumes medium-sized, white, 4–6 ft. (1.2–2 m) tall, appearing in late summer. Leaves gray-green. Although not as grand as the larger forms of the species, this cultivar is still quite showy and is among the most cold hardy of the true pampas grasses. An excellent choice for gardens of moderate size. Always hardy in zone 7, usually hardy in zone 6.

'Rosea'. Plumes mostly silver-white with a pink blush, to 8 ft. (2.4 m). Zone 8.

'Silver Comet'. White-striped pampas grass. An improvement over 'Albolineata' with more pronounced white variegation. Valued primarily for the foliage. Plumes white, medium-sized. To 8 ft. (2.4 m) in flower. Zone 8.

'Sunningdale Silver'. Widely acclaimed as the best of the larger types for the grandeur and quality of its silvery plumes. Can grow to more than 10 ft. (3 m) tall. Zone 8.

'White Feather'. Plumes large, white. Zone 8.

Cortaderia selloana 'Pumila' in mid-October in California.

Cortaderia selloana 'Silver Comet' in England.

CTENIUM
Grass family

The genus name means "comb," referring to the comblike inflorescences. Comprised of approximately 20 species native to tropical and subtropical North and South America and Africa.

Ctenium aromaticum
Toothache grass, lemon grass

Native to savannas, bogs, and wet pine barrens from Louisiana to Florida and north on the coastal plain to Virginia. Leaves mostly basal, the slender flowering stems to 4 ft. (1.2 m) tall, each ending in a comblike, slightly curved inflorescence to 6 in. (15 cm) long. All parts of the plants are aromatic, having a citruslike fragrance when crushed. Also found by some people to have analgesic properties useful in treating toothaches. A curious and delicately graceful grass suited to informal garden areas or native habitat restorations. Blooms mid to late summer, the inflorescences lasting into winter. Needs full sun, moisture. Propagate by seed or by division in spring. Zone 8.

CYMBOPOGON
Grass family

Comprised of approximately 50 clump-forming, mostly perennial species native to tropical and subtropical Africa, Asia, and Australia. Most are strongly aromatic, including citronella, *C. nardus*. Oils from these grasses are used for cooking, perfumes, herbal remedies, and insect repellents.

Cymbopogon citratus
Lemon grass

Native to southern India and Sri Lanka. The oil from this species is strongly lemon scented, and the leaves are widely used for flavoring in Southeast Asian cuisine. The plant is also quite handsome. Though too tender to survive winter in most temperate regions, it can be held over the cold season in a greenhouse or sunny window and planted out for the summer and autumn in the ground or in a decorative pot. It is delightful to savor the scent of a crushed leaf while strolling the garden on a summer evening. Clump-forming and upright, growing 2–3 ft. (60–90 cm)

tall over the course of a summer, with light green leaves to 1 in. (25 mm) wide. Needs full sun, moisture. Not particular about soils. Zone 9.

CYMOPHYLLUS
Sedge family

The genus name refers to the minutely wavy margins of the leaves. Comprised of a single eastern North American species. A long debate has raged whether this plant belongs in the genus *Carex*.

Cymophyllus fraserianus
Fraser's sedge

Named for its discoverer, John Fraser (1750–1811). This stunning North American native is rare in the wild and rarer in cultivation. Found locally in rich, sloping, upland woods and along streambanks in the Southeast. Clump-forming, with broad, flat basal leaves. Blooms May to June. The flowers are bright white, held above the foliage on stems to 15 in. (38 cm) tall. New leaves develop after flowering, eventually growing to 20 in. (50 cm) long by ¾ in. (2 cm) wide, deep green and glossy, persisting through winter. A truly ornamental sedge, worth growing for foliage or for flowers. Requires partial shade, well-drained soil with plenty of organic matter, and steady moisture for best growth. Does well on shaded slopes. Tolerates dense deciduous shade. A handsome addition to the woodland garden. Propagate by division or seed. Zone 7.

CYPERUS
Umbrella sedge (Sedge family)

The second-largest genus in the sedge family, next to *Carex*, comprised of approximately 600 species, mostly perennial, native to wet habitats mainly in the tropics and subtropics. Includes the famous Egyptian paper reed, *Cyperus papyrus*, and the infamous yellow nutsedge, *C. esculentus*, a pernicious weed in temperate gardens.

Many species require winter protection in a greenhouse, with minimum temperatures of 50°F (10°C). They also prefer constantly moist soils, and many are semi-aquatic, preferring to

Ctenium aromaticum in late June in North Carolina.

Cymbopogon citratus in Pennsylvania in late August.

Cymophyllus fraserianus flowering in native habitat in the Smoky Mountains of North Carolina in early May.

Cymophyllus fraserianus flower detail in early May.

grow in shallow water. They make excellent year-round conservatory specimens, at the edge of a pool or pond under glass. They can also be grown in a pot with the base standing in a tray of water and can be set out during warm seasons as marginals in water gardens. Their texture provides fine contrast with the broad, bold leaves of waterlilies and other aquatics and semi-aquatics. All are best in full sun.

Propagate by division in spring, by seed, or by upper stem cuttings rooted in water. The names of *Cyperus* species have undergone considerable change, and there is much confusion and uncertainty regarding the labeling of plants in cultivation.

Cyperus albostriatus
Broad-leafed umbrella sedge

Native to southern Africa. Distinct from the other umbrella sedges in having well-developed basal leaves and bracts of the inflorescence leafy and broad, to 6 in. (15 cm) long and 1 in. (25 mm) wide, with prominent longitudinal veins. The

leaves are typically dark green. Needs moist soil but does not like to be deeply submersed in water. Tolerates shade better than most and is well adapted to cultivation as a houseplant. Zone 9.

'**Variegatus**'. This name is used for at least two different variegated selections. One has dark green leaves with bright white stripes. Another has leaves nearly evenly greenish white. Both are highly ornamental, and both benefit from partial shade in hot, sunny climates. Zone 9.

Cyperus alternifolius
Umbrella sedge, umbrella-palm

Native to Madagascar. The most commonly cultivated *Cyperus*, long a favorite for use as a houseplant or in water gardens around the world. Basal leaves are lacking. The slender leafless stems grow to 3 ft. (1 m) tall, each topped by an umbrella-like spiral of up to 25 dark green bracts. The bracts are flat and narrowly leaflike, to ⅝ in. (15 mm) wide and 4–12 in. (10–30 cm) long. This species is not clearly distinguishable from *C.*

Cyperus albostriatus in a Pennsylvania greenhouse in late February.

A variegated selection of *Cyperus albostriatus* in California in mid-August.

involucratus, and many believe the two to be the same. Although the name *C. alternifolius* is long established in horticultural circles, the name *C. involucratus* is gaining favor, in which case the following cultivars are listed under it. Zone 9.

'Gracilis'. Compact and smaller in all parts, to 18 in. (45 cm) tall.

'Variegatus'. Leaves, bracts, and stems striped or entirely cream-white. Variegation somewhat unstable, occasionally reverting to green.

Cyperus eragrostis
Pale galingale

Native of tropical America, introduced to England for ornamental purposes and naturalized there in some areas. Pale green, to 24 in. (60 cm), with leaves as tall as the stem. Flowers in late summer. Inflorescence bracts relatively few. Not as showy as the umbrella-sedges, but valued for its greater cold hardiness. Grows in garden soils of steady, average moisture. Zone 8.

Cyperus giganteus
Giant papyrus

Native to Paraguay, Uruguay, and Colombia north to Honduras and the Great Antilles, also possibly native to extreme southeastern Texas. Despite the name, this species is not necessarily larger than *C. papyrus* and is similar in many respects. It differs in having fewer inflorescence

Cyperus alternifolius in the Canary Islands in early June.

Cyperus alternifolius 'Variegatus' in a New York conservatory in late May.

Cyperus involucratus in a New York greenhouse in late May.

rays, but the rays are branched and form secondary umbels. Plants labeled *C. papyrus* 'Mexico' may be a form of *C. giganteus*. Zone 9.

Cyperus haspan

Not in cultivation; plants labeled as such generally belong to *C. profiler*. The true *C. haspan* is not ornamental, but a rather slight plant with only two narrow upward-pointing inflorescence bracts. The umbels are loose and open, with up to 10 unequal rays, not globelike. It is native in North America to swamps and shallow water, mostly along the coast from Virginia to Florida and Texas, and widely distributed in tropical and subtropical regions throughout the world.

Cyperus involucratus
Umbrella sedge, umbrella-palm

Native to Africa. Nearly identical to *C. alternifolius*, but sometimes slightly taller with a few more bracts in the inflorescence. Zone 9.

Cyperus longus
Galingale

Native to coastal marshes and pondsides in England, Europe, Asia, and North Africa. Slender and upright to 3 ft. (1 m), lacking the umbel or umbrella-like inflorescences common to other *Cyperus* species. Bracts of the inflorescence few, slender, erect or ascending. Valued ornamentally for the fine-textured, almost grassy effect, and cold hardiness. Runs strongly. Zone 7.

Cyperus papyrus
Papyrus, Egyptian paper reed

Native to northern Africa. Egyptians used this species, which once grew along the Nile River, to make the paperlike papyrus they wrote upon. The stems were cut vertically into thin strips and laid parallel to each other, then another layer was laid at right angles. The resulting mat was pressed together and dried in the sun. This species is also believed to be the bulrush referred to in the Bible. It is a majestic plant, capable of

Cyperus papyrus in the Canary Islands in early June.

Cyperus profiler in a Pennsylvania greenhouse in late February.

growing 15 ft. (4.5 m) tall, though ornamental specimens are usually much shorter. Basal leaves are lacking. The stout, leafless stems are topped by inflorescences forming huge umbels 1 ft. (30 cm) wide or more, looking vaguely like giant onion flowers. The numerous rays of the inflorescence are threadlike, each ending in clusters of flower spikelets. The inflorescences are produced through the summer and are particularly beautiful when side-lit or back-lit by the sun. Spreads by stout rhizomes, but can easily be maintained as a clump. Zone 9.

Cyperus profiler
Miniature papyrus, dwarf papyrus

Native to edges of swamps and streams in eastern and southern Africa, Madagascar, and the Mascarene Islands. Very much resembles *C. papyrus* in miniature. Stems slender, to 3 ft. (1 m) tall. The inflorescence is an umbel, usually 2½–4 in. (6–10 cm) in diameter. Plants in cultivation

frequently produce sterile umbels, lacking spikelets at the ends of the rays. The rays radiate stiffly from the center, looking slightly like exploding green fireworks. Basal leaves lacking, the leaves reduced to sheaths. Runs by rhizomes but easily managed as a clump. Prefers constantly moist or wet soils. Grows well in shallow water. Zone 9.

DESCHAMPSIA
Hair grass, tussock grass (Grass family)

Named for French naturalist Louis Deschamps (1765–1842). Comprised of approximately 40 mostly perennial species of circumboreal distribution, mostly native to meadows, moorlands, upland grasslands, and open woods.

Deschampsia cespitosa
Tufted hair grass, tussock grass

The specific epithet is often misspelled *caespitosa*. A superb ornamental, valued for its neat, dark green foliage and for its inflorescences, which form billowing masses of the finest, hair-like texture. Widely distributed in temperate Europe, Asia, and North America. A cool-season grower, it prefers moist habitats, such as shores, meadows, bogs, and damp woodlands, often on heavy soils. Toward the southern extremes of its range, it is found mostly at higher, cooler elevations. Has variable foliage and flowers. Most cultivated selections derive from plants of European provenance. These perform very well in many North American regions but are not suited to the hotter zones, especially if conditions are dry.

Strictly clump-forming and tufted, with a basal tuft of narrow, dark green leaves, 1–2 ft. (30–60 cm) tall, evergreen except in the coldest zones. Flower panicles produced in late June or July, emerging in various shades of green to gold, drying to a light golden straw color and lasting through winter unless broken down by snows. To 4 ft. (1.2 m) in bloom under ideal conditions.

Long-lived and of easy culture in sun or shade, though flowering is much heavier in sun. Useful as an accent, but especially beautiful in mass, forming huge sweeping clouds of flowers that change color over the course of the seasons. Superb when contrasted against a dark background or bold-leaved companion plantings. Beautiful when dew covered on autumn mornings. Propagate the species by seed, the cultivars by division in spring or fall. The flower color differences between cultivars are subtle and are most noticeable in mass plantings. Self-sows but easily managed. Zone 4.

'Bronzeschleier' ('Bronze Veil'). Has bronze-green inflorescences. One of the best-flowering cultivars for the Pacific Northwest. Zone 4.

'Fairy's Joke'. A viviparous oddity, producing tiny young plants in place of seeds. The inflorescences are weighted down by these plantlets, sometimes rooting at point of soil contact. This cultivar is considered by some to merit recognition as *D. cespitosa* var. *vivipara*. Zone 4.

Deschampsia cespitosa in Germany in late August.

A sweep of *Deschampsia cespitosa* 'Schottland' in Pennsylvania in early August.

Deschampsia flexuosa billows over boulders in the Blue Ridge Mountains of Virginia in late July.

Deschampsia flexuosa 'Aurea' flowering in mid-May in Washington State.

Dulichium arundinaceum in the New Jersey pine barrens in late June.

'Goldgehänge' ('Golden Pendant'). Inflorescences open golden yellow, branches somewhat pendulous. Zone 4.

'Goldschleier' ('Gold Veil'). Inflorescences open golden yellow. Zone 4.

'Goldstaub' ('Gold Dust'). Inflorescences open golden yellow. Zone 4.

'Goldtau' ('Gold Dew'). Inflorescences open yellow-green. Zone 4.

'Northern Lights'. A dramatic variegated selection. Leaves with cream-white longitudinal stripes, sometimes suffused pink in cool seasons, to 10 in. (25 cm) maximum height. Rarely flowers. Zone 4.

'Schottland' ('Scotland'). Scottish tufted hair grass. As the German cultivar name implies, this selection is of Scottish origin. Leaves dark green, with light green inflorescences. Zone 4.

'Tardiflora'. Slightly later blooming than the species, flowers in late summer. Zone 4.

'Tauträger' ('Dew Carrier'). Inflorescences more slender than the type. Zone 4.

Deschampsia flexuosa
Crinkled hair grass, wavy hair grass

Native to North America and Eurasia, mostly in drier habitats in sun or in open woodlands. Densely tufted, similar to *D. cespitosa* but smaller in all its parts, usually less than 2 ft. (60 cm) tall. The inflorescences are billowy but not always as dense. The spikelets vary in color from bronze to pale greenish yellow. Of easy culture on a variety of soils in part sun or shade. One of the few grasses that grows well in dry woodland settings. A cool-season grower, flowering in midsummer. Propagate the species by seed, the cultivars by division in spring or fall. Self-sows manageably. Zone 4.

'Aurea' ('Tatra Gold'). Has yellow-green foliage, especially in early season, and comes true from seed. Flower spikelets soft bronze. Zone 4.

'Mückenschwarm' ('Fly Swarm'). Has a profusion of small, very dark spikelets. Zone 4.

DULICHIUM
Three-way sedge (Sedge family)

Comprised of one species, native to wet habitats across North America.

Dulichium arundinaceum
Three-way sedge

Native to North American swamps and margins of pools and streams, often in standing water. The bright green leaves are arranged in three distinct ranks that are evident when viewing the plant from above, hence the common name. The stems are upright, 2–3 ft. (60–90 cm) tall, with narrow leaves, and somewhat resemble bamboo. Flowers midsummer, ornamentally insignificant. Runs strongly by rhizomes, the dense colonies forming bright green ribbons venturing into shallow water. Beautifully characteristic of many eastern North American wetlands. Of easy culture in sun or part shade if provided constantly moist or wet soil. A fine addition to water gardens, providing contrast with bold-textured waterlilies and other broad-leaved plants. Propagate by seed or by division in spring. Zone 6.

ELEGIA
Restio family

Comprised of approximately 30 dioecious species native to the South African Cape region. Part of the fynbos plant community, which is characterized by natural fires, they are generally found on well-drained soils low in fertility. Variable in appearance, some species rushlike, others bearing a striking resemblance to horsetails, *Equisetum*. Cool-season growers, most active in spring after winter rains. Many are quite beautiful but little known in cultivation. They are suitable for gardens in Mediterranean and warm temperate regions.

Elegia capensis

Usually grows along streamsides and low mountain seeps from Clanwilliam to Port Elizabeth, South Africa. Clump-forming, to nearly 7 ft. (2.1 m) tall, bearing an uncanny resemblance to a giant horsetail, with dense whorls of threadlike branches spaced along the vertical stems. Brown male and female flowers on separate plants, at the tops of stems. Conspicuous papery leaf

Elegia capensis (left) and *Chondropetalum tectorum* (right) in mid-September in South Africa.

Eleocharis acicularis in shallow water along the New England coast in early August.

Elymus canadensis flowering in late June in Pennsylvania.

bracts, held closely to the stems, are a striking ornamental feature of this species. Propagate by seed. Difficult to divide as the roots do not like to be disturbed. Likes full sun and moisture. Does not do well in highly fertile soil. Best planted in spring or autumn in Mediterranean climates. An excellent seasonal container subject in areas beyond its winter cold hardiness. Zone 8.

ELEOCHARIS
Spike-rush (Sedge family)

Comprised of approximately 150 species distributed worldwide in wet soil or shallow water, many creeping by rhizomes to form dense mats. The leaves are reduced to bladeless sheaths, the stems slender and unbranched, each topped by a terminal spikelet. The unobtrusive simplicity of these plants is often overlooked, yet they can be a graceful, fine-textured presence in wet habits and in water gardens. Many look alike, and they can be difficult to tell apart. The two following species are distinct.

Eleocharis acicularis
Slender spike-rush, needle spike-rush

The species epithet means "needle-shaped," referring to the very slender stems and spikelets. Native to low ground and damp shores, often in standing water, throughout North America and in Eurasia. Tufted and creeping by rhizomes to form dense mats. Stems fine and almost hairlike, to 1 ft. (30 cm) tall, upright or lax. A graceful addition to marginal areas in water gardens, also sometimes grown in indoor aquaria. Of easy culture in sun and moist soil or shallow water. Does best in slightly acid conditions. Propagate by division in spring or by seed. Zone 5.

Eleocharis dulcis
Chinese water-chestnut, mai-tai

Though simple and attractive, this widespread native of Asia and western Africa is more often grown for the edible tubers than for ornament. Jointed cylindrical green stems are to 3/16 in. (4

Elymus magellanicus in late May in the author's Pennsylvania garden.

mm) in diameter, to 4 ft. (1.2 m) tall. The terminal spikelet to 2 in. (5 cm) long, sometimes absent. Spreads by elongated stolons that terminate in rounded tubers to 1^1/$_2$ in. (4 cm) in diameter. Eaten fresh or cooked, the tubers are the familiar white crunchy vegetable common in Chinese foods. Of easy culture in full sun and shallow water. Propagate by offsets from tubers. Zone 9.

ELYMUS
Wild rye, wheatgrass (Grass family)

Comprised of nearly 150 perennial species, clump-forming or spreading by rhizomes, native throughout temperate latitudes of the Northern and Southern Hemispheres, in a variety of habitats, including meadows, prairies, woodlands, steppes, and dunes. A few species familiar and important to gardeners, such as the blue lyme grasses, *E. arenarius* and *E. racemosus*, have been tranferred to the closely related genus *Leymus* (which see). The species below

are of minor ornamental significance except for *E. magellanicus*, which is unrivaled among grasses for the intense blue color of its foliage.

Elymus canadensis
Canada wild rye

Native along riverbanks, prairies, open ground, and often dry sandy soil over much of the United States and Canada. Clump-forming, 3–6 ft. (1–2 m) tall, flowering in mid to late summer. The inflorescences are reminiscent of cultivated rye, nodding gently and remaining attractive long into winter. The foliage is coarse-textured, usually green but sometimes glaucous blue-green. A fast-growing but somewhat short-lived prairie grass sometimes included in seed mixes to serve as a nurse crop for slower-growing prairie grasses and forbs. Of easy culture in sun on almost any soil, moist or dry. Propagates easily from seed or may be divided in spring. Self-sows, which is desirable in meadows or prairie restorations but may be a nuisance in small gardens. Zone 3.

Elymus glaucus
Blue wild rye

Native to moist or dry open thickets across northern North America. Clump-forming and densely tufted, leaves usually glaucous blue-green. Of minor ornamental value, this species is not often cultivated; however, the name *E. glaucus* hort. is often used in error in nursery catalogs and garden books to refer to *Leymus arenarius*, a running species with strongly glaucous foliage. Zone 5.

Elymus magellanicus
Magellan wheatgrass, blue wheatgrass

Native to higher elevations in South America. This tufted clump-former has the most intense blue foliage of all the grasses; other grasses traditionally considered bluish, such as *Helictotrichon sempervirens* and *Festuca glauca*, appear dull in comparison. Foliage is semi-evergreen in mild climates. Unfortunately, this cool-season grower does poorly in areas with humid summers with high night temperatures. In southern England it is prone to severe foliar rust disease. Still, the dramatic color is worth some coddling. Sharply drained soil is a necessity, especially in areas with wet winters. Light shade helps to relieve summer sulks in hot climates. Does well in coastal areas. Makes a superb container subject. Propagate by seed or by division in spring. Zone 6.

'Blue Tango'. Collected in South America.

Elymus virginicus
Virginia wild rye

A quite variable clump-forming species native to rich thickets, alluvial soils, shores, and sometimes alkaline areas over much of eastern North America. Of minor ornamental importance. Similar to *E. canadensis* but coarser and usually green-leaved, occasionally slightly glaucous, the inflorescences with less-pronounced awns. Flowers midsummer. Propagates easily by seed. Zone 3.

ERAGROSTIS
Lovegrass (Grass family)

Comprised of approximately 350 annual and perennial species of cosmopolitan distribution, many in tropical and subtropical zones.

Eragrostis curvula
Weeping lovegrass, African lovegrass

This grass is cold hardy far beyond what might be expected, since it is native to southern Africa. Strictly clump-forming and densely tufted, it forms a neat mound of very fine-textured foliage, overtopped in mid to late summer by arching, lavender-gray flower panicles, to 3 ft. (1 m) tall. Foliage is evergreen in mild climates, dying to the ground in cold zones. Leaves green in summer, often acquiring yellow-bronze tints in autumn. A subtle but graceful ornamental, this grass is useful as an accent or groundcover grouping and was widely planted for grassland stabilization and for erosion control on roadside embankments and other rights-of-way across the southern United States, where it has escaped and since become naturalized. Self-sows manageably. Propagate by seed or by division in spring. Zone 7.

Eragrostis elliottii
Elliott's lovegrass

Tony Avent of Plant Delights Nursery, who first noticed plants growing naturally on a Georgia hillside, deserves credit for bringing this strikingly beautiful North American native species into cultivation. With gray-blue leaves only $1/4$ in. (6 mm) wide, this lovegrass produces a soft-textured billowing mound up 3–4 ft. (90–120 cm) in height with equal spread. Airy flower clusters arch above the foliage in May and June, remaining attractive into winter. Prefers full sun. Very drought tolerant but requires excellent winter soil drainage. Propagates readily from seed or by division. This clumpformer self-sows readily, making it well suited for use in seed-sown mass plantings and naturalizing in appropriate places. It could serve as an alternative or replacement for the African native weeping lovegrass, *E. curvula*, which is often planted for ornament and soil stabilization along roadside rights-of-way. Zone 7, into zone 6 if soggy winter conditions are avoided.

Eragrostis spectabilis
Purple lovegrass, tumble grass

Native on sandy soil in full sun from Maine to Minnesota south to Florida, Arizona, and Mexico. In late August through September, this grass produces volumes of fine-textured flower panicles that appear like reddish purple clouds hovering just above ground level. The foliage is somewhat coarse and messy in appearance, with dull green, mostly basal leaves to $3/8$ in. (9 mm) wide. Fortunately, this is almost completely hidden once the plant comes into bloom. Overall height is less than 2 ft. (60 cm). The inflorescence color fades to soft brown by October, and the plant is fully dormant in winter. Requires full sun but is drought tolerant and does not mind sandy, infertile, or poorly drained soils. Tends to be short lived. Self-sows readily on disturbed soils in or out of the garden. Cut back soon after flowering to avoid seeding or let seed-heads remain if naturalizing in meadow gardens. Drifts or sweeps can be a beautiful addition to the late-summer land-

Eragrostis curvula in Germany in late August.

Eragrostis elliottii in early September in Pennsylvania.

Eragrostis spectabilis in eastern Pennsylvania in late August.

Eragrostis spectabilis and tickseed sunflower, *Bidens polylepis*, in a moist northern Delaware meadow in mid-September.

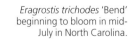

Eragrostis trichodes 'Bend' beginning to bloom in mid-July in North Carolina.

scape. In smaller gardens, the panicles show up well against gray- or silver-leaved groundcovers. Attractive with *Eupatorium hyssopifolium*. Propagates easily by seed. Zone 5.

Eragrostis trichodes
Sand lovegrass

Native to sandy barrens and open sandy woodlands from Illinois to Colorado and Texas. Much taller than *E. spectabilis*, with upright, leafy flowering stems often reaching 4 ft. (1.2 m) in height. Inflorescences in July and early August, reddish pink tinted, but not as strongly colored as those of *E. spectabilis*. Easily grown in sun on any well-drained soil. Drought tolerant. Self-sows manageably. Propagate by seed or by division in spring. Zone 5.

'Bend'. Lax-stemmed, arching under the weight of its flowers and gently leaning on neighbors in late season, usually with pleasing results. Zone 5.

ERIOPHORUM
Cotton grass (Sedge family)

The genus name means "wool bearing," referring to the woolly flower heads. Comprised of approximately 20 species native throughout northern temperate and arctic zones, all perennials, most growing in acid swamps and sphagnum bogs, often at higher elevations. These species are distinct among sedges in having numerous fine bristles extending beyond the flower spikelets to form dense tufts resembling balls of cotton. The color of the bristles varies from tawny and dull to nearly pure white. Cotton grasses are superb cut flowers but should never be picked from wild populations. Some species are clump-forming, others run by rhizomes. All require full sun, cool summers, plenty of moisture, and acid soil for best growth. Propagate by seed or by division in spring.

Eriophorum angustifolium
Common cotton grass, cotton grass

Native to bogs from Greenland across North America to Alaska south to New York, Michigan, Iowa, and Washington, common throughout the British Isles, also native to Europe and Asia. To $2^1/2$ ft. (80 cm) tall, creeping extensively by rhizomes. Bristles white. Zone 3.

Eriophorum virginicum
Virginia cotton grass

Abundantly native in swamps, bogs, and wet meadows, only in North America from Newfoundland and Quebec to Manitoba and Minnesota south through the New Jersey pine barrens to Florida and Kentucky. Tufted and clump-forming, to 3 ft. (1 m) tall. Bristles white or tawny. Tolerates warm, humid summers better than species restricted to cool climates. Zone 4.

Eriophorum virginicum growing in its native habitat in the mountains of West Virginia in mid-October.

FESTUCA
Fescue (Grass family)

Comprised of approximately 300 tufted or rhizomatous perennial species of cosmopolitan distribution, but mainly in temperate zones. Fescues are often important, fine-textured constituents of lawns; however, most ornamental garden species are tufted clump-formers valued for various shades of blue-green or glaucous-blue foliage. Most prefer full sun and sharply drained soils. They are cool-season growers, often suffering during hot, humid summer periods. Propagate the species by seed, the cultivars by division only. Individual clumps tend to be relatively short-lived, dying out in the center as they age. Plants are best renewed by division every few years. Many benefit from being cut back yearly in late winter or early spring.

Festuca amethystina
Large blue fescue

Native to central Europe. Tufted and clump-forming, to 2 ft. (60 cm) in flower. Leaves rolled and

threadlike, the foliage texture extremely fine, color varying from blue-green to intensely glaucous gray-blue. The June flowers are attractive, held well above the foliage on slender stalks. Of similar garden use to the common blue fescue, *F. glauca*, but slightly larger. Zone 4.

'Aprilgrün' ('April Green'). Leaves green. Flower stems lack the amethyst color of 'Superba'.

'Bronzeglanz'. Lightly tinted bronze.

'Klose'. Leaves olive-colored, shorter than typical. Named for German nurseryman Heinz Klose.

'Superba'. Foliage intensely blue-silver, to 1 ft. (30 cm), rivaling the best of the *F. glauca* cultivars. Flowers in June to 2 ft. (60 cm). Remarkable and outstanding for the slender amethyst-colored stalks supporting the inflorescences. The color can be vivid for about three weeks in June.

Festuca californica
California fescue

Native to dry open ground, chaparral, thickets, and open forests to approximately 5000 ft. (1500

Festuca amethystina 'Superba' in early June in Pennsylvania.

Festuca californica in mid-December in California.

Festuca glauca 'Blausilber' in Pennsylvania in late June.

m) in elevation in Oregon and in California west of the Sierra Nevada, occasionally on serpentine soils. Often found on north-facing slopes. A truly beautiful medium-sized grass, with slightly flat, blue-green or glaucous blue-gray leaves in a loose mound 2–3 ft. (60–90 cm) tall, topped by airy flower panicles anytime from April through June. A cool-season grower, fully evergreen in milder climates. Long-lived and durable. Effective as a specimen or massed for groundcover. Easily grown on a variety of soils. Fairly drought tolerant but looks best when moisture provided. Use fingers or a stiff rake to comb out occasional accumulations of old foliage. Propagate by division in spring or fall or by seed. Zone 7.

'Mayacmas Blue'. Foliage gray-blue.

'Salmon Creek'. Foliage blue-gray.

'Serpentine Blue'. Foliage intensely gray-blue, a strong bloomer. Introduced from a plant growing on a serpentine seep in Marin County, California.

Festuca glauca
Blue fescue, gray fescue

Native to southern France. Strictly clump-forming, foliage densely tufted, forming neat mounds 6–10 in. (15–25 cm) tall, topped by upright flower panicles in June. Inflorescences at first colored like the foliage, soon bleaching to light tan. Plants often look best if flowers are sheared off upon drying. A superb color accent and good container plants. A cool-season grower, it often sulks during hot, humid summers. Though it is frequently employed in groundcover masses and can be quite stunning in this manner, its short-lived nature guarantees that a fair amount of maintenance is necessary to keep plantings looking neat and uniform. Individual plants tend to die out at the center after two to four years, especially if stressed by summer heat or water-logged soils in winter. In any case, annual shearing in late winter often contributes to longer life and neater appearance. Cultivars are frequently

Festuca glauca 'Elijah Blue' in late May in Delaware.

Festuca idahoensis in mid-July in Pennsylvania.

New foliage of *Festuca glauca* 'Golden Toupee' is bright chartreuse in early May in Oregon.

Festuca glauca 'Golden Toupee' in late May in Delaware.

mislabeled in commerce, clonal cultivars are adulterated by seed-propagation, and leftover stock of all names is sometimes lumped as generic "blue fescue." It often pays to inspect plants before purchase. Below are some of the more distinct, widely grown selections. Most are reliably hardy to zone 4.

'Azurit'. Leaves blue-silver.

'Blaufink' ('Blue Finch'). Leaves silver-blue.

'Blaufuchs' ('Blue Fox'). Leaves silver-blue.

'Blauglut' ('Blue Glow'). Leaves silver-blue.

'Blausilber' ('Blue Silver'). Leaves blue-silver. One of the best primarily silver-leaved selections.

'Daeumling' ('Tom Thumb'). Compact, foliage less than 6 in. (15 cm).

'Elijah Blue'. If in doubt, choose this one. Leaves strongly silver-blue. One of the more durable and longer-lived selections.

'Frühlingsblau' ('Spring Blue'). Leaves silver-blue.

The rich sea-blue of *Festuca glauca* 'Meerblau' will be a continuing presence long after the surrounding heaths and heathers in this German garden have ceased blooming.

Festuca mairei in Germany in late August.

Festuca rubra in mid-October in California.

'Golden Toupee'. A truly unusual blue fescue, with new foliage that is not blue at all but rather a striking chartreuse. The color is most intense and longest lasting in regions with cool summer nights. In warmer, more humid regions the foliage turns to light green by summer. Less heat and drought tolerant than the glaucous blue types. Rarely tops 10 in. (30 cm) even in bloom. Zone 4.

'Meerblau' ('Sea Blue'). Leaves rich sea-blue, with some green hues, too. Distinct and attractive.

'Seeigel' ('Sea Urchin'). Leaves blue-green.

'Silberreiher' ('Silver Egret'). Leaves blue-silver.

'Solling'. Leaves silver-gray.

Festuca idahoensis
Idaho fescue, blue bunchgrass

Despite the common name, this species is native to open woods and rocky slopes from British Columbia to Alberta, south to central California and Colorado. A cool-season grower, clump-forming, densely tufted and longer-lived than *F. glauca*. Trial plants at Longwood Gardens have persisted without center dieback for nearly a decade without division and have appeared more tolerant of wet winter soils. Foliage blue-green to silver-blue, to 14 in. (35 cm) tall. Propagate by division or seed. Zone 5.

Festuca mairei
Atlas fescue

Native to the Atlas Mountains of Morocco, at elevations to 7500 ft. (2300 m). Well known to German grass pioneer Karl Foerster, this unique and useful medium-sized grass is handsome yet still generally underappreciated. It makes a neat mound of flat, gray-green foliage 2– 2$^1/_2$ ft. (60–80 cm) tall, topped by very slender flower panicles in June. A cool-season grower, but more tolerant of hot summers than many fescues. Slow-growing but durable and long-lived. Fully evergreen in milder climates. Use fingers or a stiff rake to comb out occasional accumulations of old foliage. Prefers full sun. Propagate by division in spring or by seed. Zone 5.

Festuca ovina
Sheep's fescue

Widespread in temperate zones, but not important to ornamental gardens. The common blue garden fescues belong to *F. glauca*.

Festuca rubra
Creeping red fescue

A widespread native throughout Europe and North America. Runs strongly by rhizomes and is best known for the many selections that have been developed for use as mown turf grasses. These green-leaved varieties generally require generous moisture for good growth, and many are escaped and naturalized. Bluish-leaved selections from native California populations have proved fairly drought tolerant and show promise as ornamental groundcovers for drier climates. Full sun. Propagate by division. Zone 5.

'Jughandle'. This California selection is compact, with bluish leaves.

'Molate'. Leaves bluish. This California selection is heat and drought tolerant.

Festuca valesiaca
Wallis fescue

Native to Europe. Similar in most practical respects to the common blue fescue. Represented in cultivation mostly by the following selection. Zone 5.

'Glaucantha'. Leaves blue-green, fine textured, less than 6 in. (15 cm) tall.

GLYCERIA
Manna grass, sweet grass (Grass family)

The genus name means "sweet," referring to the sweetness of the grain, which is attractive to waterfowl, and of the foliage, which is favored by grazing livestock. Comprised of nearly 40 perennial species, native to wet places in temperate zones throughout the world. Most are strongly rhizomatous.

Glyceria maxima
Manna grass, great water grass

Native to wet soils and shallow water in marshes and at the edges of rivers, ponds, and lakes in Europe and temperate Asia. Green-leaved, with erect, airy flower panicles 6–8 ft. (2–2.4 m) tall, appearing mid to late summer. Spreads aggressively by stout rhizomes. Attractive to waterfowl. Requires full sun and moisture. Not particular about soils. Usually grown for the following cultivar. Zone 6.

Glyceria maxima 'Variegata' in mid-May in Washington State.

Glyceria obtusa seeds are rich brown in mid-September in coastal New Jersey.

'Variegata'. Variegated manna grass. Has bright cream-yellow-striped leaves, often tinted pink during cool periods in spring and autumn. To only 20 in. (50 cm) tall, and rarely flowering. Not as aggressive a runner as the species, especially in drier soils, but still strong enough to overpower companions in a flower border. Best used in garden sites that offer natural checks, such as pond edges and streambanks. Easily tolerates poorly drained soils or standing water. Properly sited, this grass can provide an attractive trouble-free mass of brightly colored foliage. Also effective mixed with other plants in container displays. Deciduous in winter, the foliage becoming an unkempt, light brown mass. Propagate by division in spring or fall. Cut back yearly. Zone 5.

Glyceria obtusa
Blunt manna grass
Native to bogs and marshy places from Nova Scotia south along the coast through the New Jersey pine barrens to North Carolina. Interesting for the bright yellow-green color of its foliage and for its erect, dense flower panicles, 2–3 ft. (60–90 cm) tall, which turn deep brown by late summer. An excellent food source for native waterfowl. Runs by rhizomes. Propagate by seed or by division in spring. Zone 6.

HAKONECHLOA
Hakone grass (Grass family)
Comprised of one highly ornamental species native to wet, rocky cliffs in the mountains of Japan's main island, Honshu, including the region near Mount Hakone, from which the genus name is derived.

Hakonechloa macra
Hakone grass, urahagusa
The graceful, arching stems of this slow spreader form loose, cascading mounds 1–3 ft. (30–90 cm) tall. The soft foliage is rich green and reminiscent of bamboo. Plants spread by rhizomes and stolons, enough to warrant use as a groundcover but never invasive. In mid to late summer inflorescences appear between the leaves and are subtly attractive. Although a warm-season

Hakonechloa macra in mid-June in Pennsylvania.

Hakonechloa macra
'Albovariegata' in
Pennsylvania in early June.

Hakonechloa macra 'All Gold'
in mid-June in Pennsylvania.

Hakonechloa macra
'Aureola' in mid-October
in full sun in Japan.

Hakonechloa macra 'Aureola' in part shade in late May in Connecticut.

grower, Hakone grass requires a cool, moist environment for best growth. In warm, dry climates it should be grown in substantial shade. In cooler moist climates, it is luxuriant even in nearly full sun. It turns exquisite copper-orange tones in autumn. Superb for accent, groundcover or sweeps, and container subjects. All require moist, organic, well-drained soils. Best divided or transplanted in spring. A fungal blight afflicting the genus has been observed on plants growing in Maryland. Zone 4.

'Albovariegata' ('Albostriata'). White-variegated Hakone grass. Similar to the species except the rich green foliage is accented by fine longitudinal white stripes. Larger and much more vigorous than 'Aureola', growing 3 ft. (1 m) tall in zone 6. Also more tolerant of warm, sunny sites, including gardens in the southeastern United States. Easy to propagate by division in spring. Introduced to the West from the private garden of Masato Yokoi, a Japanese specialist in variegated plants. Zone 4.

'All Gold'. This introduction has all-gold leaves, without any green stripes. Growth rate and size are similar to those of 'Aureola'. Requires partial shade in warm climates. Zone 6.

'Aureola' ('Albo-aurea'). Golden-variegated Hakone grass. The leaves are almost entirely variegated, with only a few slender stripes of green remaining, especially at the margins. When grown in deep shade, the variegation is a lime green. When grown in part sun in warm regions, such as the eastern United States, the variegation is a strong golden yellow. When grown in sun in cool climates, such as England and the Pacific Northwest, the variegation is more cream-white than yellow. Cool temperatures in spring and in autumn, especially, induce beautiful suffusions of pink and red to the foliage. 'Aureola' is shorter, to 14 in. (35 cm), much slower growing, and less easy to propagate than the green-leaved form. It makes a striking color accent or container subject. Zone 6.

'Beni Fuchi'. Foliage is chocolate-brown in summer and red in autumn, especially toward the tips. There is more than one clone in Japan with these characteristics. Still rare in cultivation outside Japan. Zone 5.

HELICTOTRICHON
Oat grass (Grass family)
The genus name means "twisted hair," referring to the shape of the awn. Includes nearly 100 perennial species, mostly native to dry hillsides, meadows, and margins of woods in temperate Eurasia, but extending to other temperate regions throughout the world, including North America. Only the following species is an important ornamental.

Helictotrichon sempervirens
Blue oat grass
A native of the western Mediterranean region. The best of the medium-sized blue-leaved grasses. Strictly clump-forming, producing a dense tuft of erect, silver-blue foliage to 2^1/$_2$ ft. (80 cm) tall, evergreen in mild climates and semi-evergreen even in cold climates. Delicate inflorescences appear in late spring, held more than 2

Helictotrichon sempervirens in late May in the author's Pennsylvania garden.

Hesperostipa spartea in a Minnesota prairie in mid-June.

Helictotrichon sempervirens provides the focal point in this modern border featuring a classically styled urn and recycled concrete paving in Washington State in mid-August.

ft. (60 cm) above the foliage on slender, arching stems. A cool-season grower with flowering best if plants are provided fertile, well-drained soil and if spring conditions are cool and steadily moist. Flowering is often sparse if conditions are hot and humid; however, this grass is worth growing just for the foliage. Susceptible to disfiguring foliar rusts if late-summer humidity is high, especially if soils are poorly drained. Poor winter drainage can cause root rot. Superb as a specimen, color accent, or container specimen. Propagate the species by seed, the cultivars by division in spring. Zone 4.

'Pendula'. Heavy blooming, inflorescence more nodding than the species.

'Robust'. Rust-resistant.

'Saphirsprudel' ('Sapphire Fountain'). Foliage a bright steel blue. Improved rust-resistance.

HESPEROSTIPA
Needle grass (Grass family)
The genus name means "western *Stipa*." Comprised of four perennial North American species, segregated from *Stipa*, all with conspicuous, long awns.

Hesperostipa spartea
Porcupine grass
Native to open hillsides and prairies in central North America. Clump-forming, upright, to 3 ft. (1 m) tall in flower, the inflorescences nodding at the tops of the culms. Remarkable for the flowing awns, to 8 in. (20 cm) long. Threadlike and translucent, they shimmer and sparkle in strong sun as breezes blow across the surface of the prairie. Of easy culture in full sun on most soils of average moisture. Propagate by seed. Self-sows manageably. Zone 3.

HIEROCHLOE
Holy grass, sweet grass (Grass family)
The genus name means "sacred grass." The fragrant leaves have been used to scent churches on holy days and as incense by Native Americans. Scarcely ornamental from a visual standpoint, but perhaps of interest to those who consider scent an ornamental aspect of the garden.

Hierochloe occidentalis
California sweet grass
Native in moist and dry coniferous forests in California and Washington. Crushed leaves have a wonderfully sweet fragrance. Upright, to 3 ft. (1 m) in flower, running by rhizomes. Prefers light or dense shade and moisture. Propagate by seed or division. Zone 7.

Hierochloe odorata
Vanilla grass, sweet grass
Native to wet sites and meadows in North America and Eurasia. Upright, to 2 ft. (60 cm) in flower, running aggressively by rhizomes. Of easy culture in sun or part shade on moist soils. Propagate by seed or division. Crushed leaves have a strong, sweet fragrance. Zone 4.

HOLCUS
Grass family
The genus name means "sorghum." Comprised of six annual and perennial species native to woods and open grasslands in Europe, temperate Asia, and Africa.

Holcus lanatus
Velvet grass, Yorkshire fog
Native to moist or dry meadows and open woodlands throughout the British Isles, in Europe, temperate Asia, and Africa, and introduced and naturalized in North and South America. The leaves and stems are densely covered with fine hairs. Strictly clump-forming, producing an erect flower panicle to 3 ft. (1 m) in spring or early summer, opens white to pale green, often with pink or purple tints, and dries narrower but fluffy and cream-white. Easy to grow in full sun on any soil, but self-sows readily. A cool-season grower, often semidormant in midsummer. The melic grasses, particularly *Melica ciliata*, are similar in producing fluffy white inflorescences but are more easily managed in the garden. Zone 5.

Holcus lanatus flowering in late June in coastal Massachusetts.

Holcus mollis 'Variegatus' in early October in New Zealand.

Holcus mollis
Creeping soft grass

Native to woods and poor grasslands in Europe, especially on acid soils. Superficially similar to *H. lanatus* but not quite as soft-hairy and creeping extensively by rhizomes. Self-sows. Because of its aggressive spread, the green-leaved species form is rarely cultivated for ornament.

'Variegatus' ('Albovariegatus'). Leaves heavily striped white. Creeping by rhizomes, but manageable. Foliage usually less than 8 in. (20 cm) tall, at its best in cool spring and autumn weather. Benefits from midsummer shearing in hot, humid climates. Not a strong bloomer. Grow in full sun in cool climates or part shade in warmer zones. Quite showy and much less vigorous than the species. Makes a fine, near-white groundcover in cool climates. Propagate by division in spring or fall. Zone 6.

Hordeum jubatum in early August along the Maine coast.

HORDEUM
Barley (Grass family)

Comprised of approximately 40 annual and perennial species distributed throughout temperate regions of the world, mostly on dry soils. Includes cultivated barley, *H. vulgare*, an extremely important cereal crop valued for its short growing season and salt tolerance. Only *H. jubatum* is cultivated for ornament.

Hordeum jubatum
Foxtail barley

The most ornamental of the wild barleys, native to meadows and open ground from Alaska to Newfoundland south to Maryland, Texas, California, and Mexico, and widely introduced and naturalized elsewhere. Though a perennial, this species is often short-lived, behaving more like an annual in the garden. Its long-awned, salmon-pink inflorescences are unquestionably showy and make superb cut flowers, but this species self-sows so prolifically it should be introduced only with caution. It is a noxious weed in irrigated pastures in the western United States. A cool-season grower to 2^{1}/$_{2}$ ft. (80 cm) tall, flowering in June and July, and usually unkempt later in the season. Easily grown from seed in full sun on any soil, even on salt-laden coastal sands. Zone 4.

HYSTRIX
Bottle-brush grass (Grass family)

The genus name means "porcupine," referring to the long-awned, bristlelike flower spikes. Includes up to nine perennial species native to woodlands and meadows in North America, temperate Asia, and New Zealand. Closely related to and sometimes included in *Elymus*.

Hystrix patula
Bottle-brush grass

Native to moist or rocky woods in eastern North America. Clump-forming, upright, to 3 ft. (1 m) tall. Grown for the attractive bottlebrush-like inflorescences, to 6 in. (15 cm) long, first appearing in mid-June and produced intermittently through August, after rains. Opening green, bleaching to

Hystrix patula in native habitat at a deciduous woodland edge in Missouri in early June.

Hystrix patula inflorescence resembles a bottlebrush.

tan, they often remain attractive into autumn, when the deciduous forest foliage is at its color peak. Useful fresh or dried for cut flower arrangements. One of relatively few true grasses adapted to dry shaded conditions. Responds well to moist fertile garden soils but suffers in hot sun except in colder climates. Best in informal settings. The foliage is coarsely textured, and though the flowers are dramatic up close, they are easily lost in the overall landscape picture. Self-sows but easily managed. Ideal for naturalizing in shaded gardens. Propagate by seed. Zone 4.

IMPERATA
Grass family
Comprised of eight rhizomatous perennial species, native throughout the tropics, extending to warm temperate regions. *Imperata cylindrica* has two botanical varieties (or phases), one a mild-mannered ornamental, the other a serious pest in tropical and subtropical climates. Var. *koenigii*, common to lowlands in Japan, China, Korea, and Manchuria, represents the temperate

Imperata cylindrica var. *koenigii* 'Red Baron' in Pennsylvania in mid-September.

phase of the species and is sufficiently distinct from the tropical phase that it has been sometimes designated a separate species, *I. koenigii*. It spreads at a moderate pace by rhizomes. Var. *major* represents the larger, more aggressive tropical phase of the species, which is notoriously invasive in warm tropical and subtropical climates. This variety is the primary target of legislation restricting the sale of *I. cylindrica* in the United States.

Imperata cylindrica var. *koenigii* 'Red Baron'
Japanese blood grass

Also known as 'Rubra'. This red-leaved garden form has been well known for more than a century in Japan (although certainly not as 'Red Baron', a name coined by Kurt Bluemel), where it is usually grown in shallow containers as a companion plant to specimen bonsai. It spreads very slowly by shallow rhizomes. Leaves are upright, to 20 in. (50 cm), emerging green at the base and red at the tips in spring, the color increasing over summer, becoming solid and intense in later summer and autumn. Occasional reversions to solid green are easily removed and show no change in other characteristics, such as size or rate of spread. Color fades with hard frosts. Winter interest is negligible, and plants are best cut to the ground. Rarely blooms, but when present inflorescences are narrow, silky white, to 2 ft. (60 cm) tall. Grows most luxuriant in moist, fertile soils in full sun. Drought tolerant once established and tough enough for groundcover use in challenging sites, such as parking lots and traffic islands. A strong color accent, dramatic in sweeps and masses. Propagate by division and transplant in spring. Zone 6.

ISOLEPIS
Sedge family

Includes approximately 30 species of cosmopolitan distribution, mostly in moist habitats. Closely related to and sometimes included in *Scirpus*. Only the following species is commonly grown in gardens.

Isolepis cernua in California in late November.

Isolepis cernua
Fiber-optics plant, mop-sedge

Native in the British Isles to open peaty or sandy soils, often near the coast. Also native to Europe and northern Africa. Forms an extremely dense, moplike tuft of fine green stems. Similar in appearance to the spike-rushes, *Eleocharis*, having small terminal spikes. Interesting when grown in a pot, elevated planter, or between rocks at water's edge, highlighting the plant's pendent, spilling form. Easily grown in well-drained soil with moisture, in sun or part shade. Often grown under glass, where it remains fully evergreen. Propagate by division or seed. Zone 8.

JUNCUS
Rush (Rush family)

Comprised of approximately 200 mostly perennial, rhizomatous species, native to moist or wet habitats mainly through the world's temperate zones. The leaves are most often cylindrical and

Juncus effusus flowering in native habitat in northern Delaware in early June.

Juncus inflexus 'Afro' in mid-August in Pennsylvania.

green. Flowers are subtle and of minor ornamental value. Rushes are most beautiful in their strong, vertical form and fine texture, providing stunning contrast to broad-leaved companions in moist and wet garden areas and in native landscapes. Although they generally form clumps, they also spread by rhizomes and tend to self-sow freely, sometimes requiring control in small-scale designs. In cold climates, they often die to the ground each year and are renewed by fresh, clean growth in spring. In milder climates, old stems tend to accumulate and gradually discolor, resulting in messy appearance. Occasional cutting to the ground is recommended. Propagate by division in spring or by seed.

Juncus effusus
Common rush, soft rush

Widely native in moist or wet sunny habitats in temperate regions, including Europe and North America. A striking, architecturally interesting

plant with dark forest-green stems, upright and arching in a broad fan, to 4 ft. (1.2 m) in height. This species has been employed in Japan for centuries to make the split-rush mats called tatami. The cold hardiness varies between plants of different provenance, but the hardiest are reliable in zone 4.

'Carman's Japanese'. Selected by Ed Carman of California. Medium-green stems and slightly finer texture than the type. Zone 6.

'Cuckoo'. Has longitudinal gold stripes. A vigorous grower.

'Spiralis'. Stems dark green, twisted, and spiraled. Less than 14 in. (35 cm) tall. Often retains twisted character when grown from seed. Zone 5.

Juncus inflexus
Hard rush

Widely native in moist or wet sunny habitats in temperate regions, including Europe and North America. The stems are more narrowly upright

and gray-green than those of the common rush, 2–4 ft. (60–120 cm) tall. Zone 6.

'**Afro**'. Stems gray-green, twisted, and spiraled. Similar in appearance to *J. effusus* 'Spiralis' but more vigorous and drought tolerant. Less than 14 in. (35 cm) tall. Usually retains twisted character when grown from seed. Zone 6.

'**Lovesick Blues**'. Weeping blue rush. Originating as a seedling growing near plants of the usually upright *J. inflexus*, 'Lovesick Blues' produces a graceful fountain of blue-green foliage that is wider than high. Grows to 14 in. (35 mm) tall. Zone 4.

Juncus patens
California gray rush

Native to marshy places in California and Oregon. Differs from the common rush mostly in stem color, which is conspicuously gray-green to gray-blue, and in the stiffer, more vertical stance. To 2 ft. (60 cm). More heat and drought tolerant than the common rush. Prefers full sun, best on moist soil or in shallow water. Zone 7.

'**Carman's Gray**'. Selected by Ed Carman of California. Fairly typical of the species. Zone 7.

Juncus inflexus 'Lovesick Blues' in mid-July in North Carolina.

Juncus effusus 'Spiralis' in Pennsylvania in early June.

Juncus patens in early May in southern California.

Koeleria macrantha in early June in Missouri.

Koeleria glauca in mid-July in Washington State.

Leymus arenarius 'Blue Dune' in Pennsylvania in mid-October.

KOELERIA
Hair grass (Grass family)

Named for botanist G. L. Koeler (1765–1806), who specialized in grasses. Comprised of approximately 30 annual and perennial species native to temperate North America and Eurasia. Only the two below are significant ornamentals, and these are so similar to each other, except for foliage color, that they are sometimes included in the same species, *K. macrantha*. They are cool-season growers, usually flowering in June and then going partly or fully dormant in areas where summers are hot and humid. In cooler climates they remain presentable through autumn. They tend to be short-lived perennials. Blooming earlier than many grasses, they make fine companions for flowering perennials. In hot climates, organize borders to mask the grasses' summer dormancy. Ideal for naturalizing in a meadow garden. Easily grown in full sun on moist or moderately dry soils. Propagate by seed or by division in spring. Cold hardiness varies with seed provenance.

Koeleria glauca
Blue hair grass

Native to Europe and northern temperate Asia, particularly on sandy soils. To 2 ft. (60 cm) tall in bloom. Leaves strongly greenish blue. Zone 6.

Koeleria macrantha
June grass, crested hair grass

Native to prairies and open woods over much of the western, central, and northeastern United States. Also native to temperate Europe and Asia. To 2 ft. (60 cm) tall in bloom. Leaves medium to bright green. Plants of northern prairie provenance are cold hardy to zone 4, others to zone 6.

LEYMUS
Wild rye, lyme grass (Grass family)

Comprised of approximately 40 perennial species, native to sands, dunes, and other saline or alkaline habitats, stony slopes, and steppes, mostly in northern temperate zones. Includes many species formerly assigned to *Elymus*.

Leymus arenarius in Germany in late August.

Leymus arenarius
Sea lyme grass, European dune grass

Native on shifting sands and dunes around the coasts of the British Isles, northern and western Europe. Long popular with gardeners for the bluish foliage and a favorite of garden designer Gertrude Jekyll. Spreads aggressively by stout rhizomes. Stems erect or lax, 3–4 ft. (1–1.2 m) tall in bloom. Inflorescence a narrow spike, at first colored like the leaves, drying to light beige, not ornamental. Appearance is often improved by cutting plants back after flowering, ensuring a flush of new growth for the autumn garden. Leaves flat, to ¹/₂ in. (12 mm) wide. All plants are distinctly glaucous. Foliage attractive year-round in mild climates. A cool-season grower, but fairly tolerant of warm summers and above-average humidity. The running growth habit is pronounced in looser soils but can be contained with moderate effort. Useful as a groundcover, and often stunning as a color accent, especially with deep blue or purple flowers or maroon foliage. Of easy culture in any soil, in full sun or light shade. Extremely drought tolerant and fairly salt tolerant, adapted to use in traffic is-

lands and other challenging urban sites. Best propagated by division in spring. Often confused with the similar-looking *L. racemosus*. Zone 4.

'Blue Dune'. Especially blue and drought tolerant.

'Findhorn'. Compact, shorter growing.

Leymus cinereus
Gray wild rye, basin wild rye

Native to meadows, canyons, streamsides, sagebrush scrub, and open woodland from Minnesota to British Columbia south to Colorado, Nevada, and California, typically at higher elevations than *L. condensatus*. Stems and foliage gray-green, erect or slightly lax, to 6–8 ft. (2–2.4 m) tall in bloom. Clump-forming or spreading very slowly by rhizomes. Mostly evergreen in mild climates. Perhaps too large for modest-sized gardens, best in large drifts or sweeps in broad meadows or clearings. Prefers full sun, cool summer night temperatures, low humidity. Grows well in northern continental Europe. Drought tolerant. Propagate by seed or by division in spring. Zone 7.

Leymus cinereus in mid-June in California.

Leymus condensatus in mid-June in coastal California scrub.

A young plant of *Leymus condensatus* 'Canyon Prince' in mid-June in California.

Leymus condensatus
Giant wild rye

Native to sands and dunes, rocky slopes, and moist ravines along the southern California coast to San Diego and on the adjacent Channel Islands. Clump-forming or spreading slowly by rhizomes. Mostly evergreen in mild climates. Typically green-leaved, the largest plants growing to 9 ft. (2.7 m) tall in bloom. Inflorescences narrowly cylindrical, appearing in June. Needs full sun, drought tolerant. Bold and somewhat coarsely textured. Propagates readily by seed or division in spring. Zone 7.

'Canyon Prince'. A handsome introduction from a collection of native material from Prince Island, one of the Channel Islands off the southern California coast. Foliage flushed green at first, becoming extremely silver-blue on maturing. Shorter than the type, growing 4 ft. (1.2 m) tall in flower. Spreads steadily by rhizomes, but not invasive. Propagate by division in spring. Zone 7.

Leymus mollis
American dune grass, sea lyme grass

Native to sand dunes along coasts, from Alaska to Greenland south to New York and central California, also along the Great Lakes, and from Siberia to Japan. Similar in most respects to *L. arenarius* but foliage usually bluish green, less glaucous, much less frequently cultivated for ornament. Zone 4.

Leymus racemosus
Giant blue wild rye, Volga wild rye

This Eurasian native is so similar in appearance and growth habit to *L. arenarius* that the two are frequently confused in gardens. Despite one of its common names, this wild rye is not appreciably larger than *L. arenarius*. The foliage may be very slightly wider but is not necessarily bluer, and the plant grows to the same maximum blooming height of 4 ft. (1.2 m). All cultural details and design applicability are the same as for *L. arenarius*. Zone 4.

'Glaucus'. A superfluous name applied to this typically glaucous-leaved species.

Leymus racemosus in Pennsylvania in late July.

LUZULA
Wood-rush (Rush family)

Comprised of approximately 80 mostly perennial species of cosmopolitan distribution but mainly in cold temperate regions of the Northern Hemisphere. Common to dry or moist woodland environments, as the common name implies. The plants are clump-forming or spreading by rhizomes. They are grown mostly for their foliage, which is often lustrous and evergreen, sometimes variegated, and for their durability as groundcovers in woodland gardens and on various soil types. Many wood-rushes have distinct whitish hairs along their leaf margins. All can be propagated by division in spring or early autumn, the species also by seed.

Luzula acuminata
Hairy wood-rush

Native to woods, clearings, and bluffs in North America from Canada south to upland Georgia west to Illinois and South Dakota. Basal leaves

Luzula acuminata in mid-July in the author's Pennsylvania garden.

Luzula nivea 'Schneehäschen' in mid-July in England.

Luzula sylvatica in Pennsylvania in early June.

Luzula sylvatica 'Marginata' flowering in early May in eastern Pennsylvania.

deep green and lustrous, broad, to $^1/_2$ in. (12 mm) wide, hairy at margins, becoming bronzed but remaining evergreen through winter. Inflorescences in April and May, to 14 in. (35 cm) tall, the umbels simple and unbranched, the flowers brownish. An attractive, slowly rhizomatous woodland groundcover. Spreads much less vigorously than the European *L. sylvatica*. Does not tolerate dense deciduous shade. Grows well in moist to moderately dry conditions. Not particular about soils. Zone 4.

Luzula nivea
Snowy wood-rush, snow rush

Native to central and southern Europe into the Alps. Loosely tufted, slowly rhizomatous, basal leaves narrow, to $^3/_{16}$ in. (4 mm) wide, green, hairy. Foliage evergreen in milder climates. Inflorescences to 2 ft. (60 cm), flower clusters dense, off-white to near white, becoming pendulous. Attractive in mass. A useful groundcover for sun or part shade. Of easy culture on most soils, moist or moderately dry. Zone 6.

'Schneehäschen' ('Little Snow Hare'). Flower heads near-white. Zone 6.

'Snowbird'. Flower heads near-white. Zone 6.

Luzula sylvatica
Greater wood-rush

Native to oak woodlands, open moorlands, streamsides, and other acid habitats in the British Isles and in western, central, and southern Europe; the Caucasus; and Turkey. The largest and finest wood-rush for groundcover use, especially in shaded settings. Forms large tussocks and spreads strongly by rhizomes, eventually making a virtually weed-proof mass. Basal leaves to $^3/_4$ in. (2 cm) wide, dark green and glossy, hair especially at margins. Foliage evergreen in milder climates, semi-evergreen through zone 6. Flowers in early May, in light green masses to 2 ft. (60 cm) tall. An excellent companion for ferns, woodland wildflowers, and shrubs. Easy to grow on most soils, including heavy clays. Prefers moisture but very drought tolerant. Zone 4.

'Aurea'. Leaves yellow-green. Zone 6.

'Höhe Tatra' ('High Tatra'). Leaves green. From the Tatra Mountains of Europe. Zone 5.

'Marginata'. The best garden wood-rush. The dark green glossy leaves, to $^5/_8$ in. (15 mm) wide, have cream-white edging $^1/_{32}$ in. (1 mm) wide. The overall effect is crisp and refined. A much underappreciated woodland groundcover. Zone 4.

'Tauernpass'. Compact with broad leaves. Zone 6.

'Woodsman' ('Wäldler'). Leaves light green. Zone 6.

MELICA
Melic (Grass family)

Comprised of approximately 70 perennial species, native to woodland shade and dry slopes in temperate regions throughout the world excluding Australia. Melic grasses are cool-season growers, adding their delightful, showy cream-white flowers to the garden in spring, then mostly going dormant or semidormant in summer. Foliage is generally coarse and unremarkable, and it is best to plan for other plantings to mask it, especially in dormancy. Partly for this reason, the more compact *M. ciliata* is a superior, more manageable garden plant than the taller *M. altissima*, which is no showier in bloom and less attractive later. A few California natives, such as *M. imperfecta*, are worth exploring for use in regional gardens in hot, dry climates. Summer-dormant plants may be cut back to the ground. Propagation by seed is usually best. Divide or transplant in spring.

Melica ciliata
Hairy melic grass, silky-spike melic

Native to Europe, northern Africa, and southwestern Asia. The showiest, most manageable melic grass. Leaves mostly basal, the flowering stems rising above and arching over the foliage to 30 ft. (9 m). The narrow flower panicles are silky-white, fading to cream, useful for bouquets if cut before fully open. A delightful addition to the spring garden. Compact and suited to smaller spaces, or effective in sweeps and masses. Prefers

Melica ciliata in early June in Pennsylvania.

Melica imperfecta with poppies in late February in a California meadow.

sun or light shade, moist or moderately dry soil. At least partly summer dormant in hot climates. Individual plants are often relatively short lived. Self-sows pleasantly. Zone 6.

Melica imperfecta
Coast range melic, foothill melic

Native to dry hillsides, chaparral, and open woodlands at low and moderate elevations in the coastal ranges of California. Foliage tufted, mostly basal. To 2 ft. (60 cm) tall in flower. Flower panicles up to 12 in. (35 cm) long, narrow, cream-white. Summer dormant if dry, but turns green quickly with winter rains, attractive in early spring. Ideal for meadow gardens. Zone 8.

MERXMUELLERA
Grass family

Named for German botanist Hermann Merxmüller (1920–1988). Comprised of 16 species native to open habitats in southern and southwestern Africa.

Merxmuellera macowanii

Native to southern Africa. A large, tussock-forming perennial to 5 ft. (1.5 m) in bloom. Inflorescences arching gracefully over the blue-green, fine-textured foliage. Evergreen in mild climates. Though little known in cultivation, this beautiful species has been cultivated in the grass garden at the Royal Botanic Gardens, Kew, England, for several years. It deserves wider attention. Zone 8.

MILIUM
Millet (Grass family)

Includes six annual and perennial species native to temperate woodlands in Eurasia and North America.

Milium effusum
Wood millet

A widespread native of damp or rocky woods in northeastern North America, damp oak and beech woods in the British Isles and Europe, and

Merxmuellera macowanii in mid-August in England.

Milium effusum 'Aureum' in late May in Connecticut.

moist mountainous woods in Japan. A pronounced cool-season grower, as evidenced by habitat preference. Only the golden form is important in gardens.

'Aureum'. Bowles' golden grass, golden wood millet. The new spring foliage is among the brightest chartreuse-yellow of all garden plants. Makes a superb color companion to spring-blooming flowers. This cool-season, woodland plant is at its best in light shade in cooler climates, and always best in spring. The foliage darkens to light green by summer and in hotter climates it goes partly dormant in summer. Heavier shade relieves summer stress but diminishes the vibrancy of the spring foliage color. 'Aureum' is smaller than the species, the foliage rarely topping 18 in. (45 cm). The open flower panicles are sparsely produced. Self-sows mildly, and seedlings usually have yellow leaves, though there may be some variation. Tolerant of a range of soils, but appreciates moisture. Propagate by division. Zone 6.

MISCANTHUS
Eulalia, Japanese silver grass
(Grass family)

Comprised of approximately 20 usually large perennial species native to marshes, slopes, mountainsides, and other open habitats, mainly in eastern Asia, but extending west into Africa. They naturalize in a diversity of habitats and are especially competitive in moist, sunny environments in warm temperate regions; however, in cool climates, such as England, where the growing season lacks the warmth and duration of sun required for prolific flowering and seed development, they pose no threat. Conditions in the southeastern United States most closely approximate ideal conditions for miscanthus, and it is here, especially near moist, sunny bottomlands, that caution is warranted.

Miscanthus are late-starting in spring but grow strongly in summer heat. They are very tolerant of poorly drained soils with low aeration and require no fertilization except on the poorest

Miscanthus 'Giganteus' in early August in Maryland.

Miscanthus 'Giganteus' in mid-October in Maryland.

sands. All species and most cultivars prefer full sun sites. They bloom from midsummer through autumn. The flowers usually remain attractive through winter. Cultivated selections can be used as specimen focal points as well as for massing and screening. Those with variegated leaves are excellent in decorative containers. Most miscanthus make superb cut flowers. Many can be stunning when placed at the edges of pools and ponds. Newer selections offer significant autumn foliage color and are graceful additions to the winter garden.

The genus includes clump-formers and strongly rhizomatous species. Individual plants live for many years, but older clumps eventually die out in their centers and should be renewed by taking divisions from the perimeter of the clump in spring or early summer. Propagate the species by seed. Cold hardiness varies considerably between species and cultivars.

Miscanthus floridulus
Tokiwa susuki

This speces has rarely, if ever, been grown for ornament in Western gardens; but this name has often been erroneously applied to a superficially similar, commonly cultivated clonal cultivar that has the tall stature and clump-forming habit of this species and the awnless florets typical of *M. sacchariflorus*.

Miscanthus 'Giganteus'
Giant miscanthus

Although frequently listed as belonging to *M. floridulus*, *M. sacchariflorus*, or *M. sinensis*, this venerable cultivar is of obscure garden origin, possibly a hybrid, but certainly a great garden plant. Upright in form, with a maximum height approaching 10 ft. (3 m). The 1-in. (25-mm) wide leaves are deep green with the white midvein common to most miscanthus. The leaves are

Miscanthus 'Purpurascens' in early September in Washington, D.C.

Miscanthus 'Purpurascens' fall foliage in full sun in early October in Pennsylvania.

pendent, giving the overall effect of a large fountain. Mostly clump-forming, only slightly rhizomatous. Blooms very late summer or not at all in short growing seasons. Inflorescences open with pink tints, quickly turning silver on drying. The shortest foliage, to 3 ft. (1 m), frequently turns brown or dies in late summer, so it is often best to place companion plantings in front to mask this. Does well at water's edge. Generally does not self-sow. Propagate by division. Zone 4.

Miscanthus 'Herbstfeuer' ('Autumn Fire')

Similar to *M.* 'Purpurascens' but shorter and slower growing. Of obscure parentage, possibly a hybrid, but certainly not *M. sinensis*. Zone 5.

Miscanthus 'Little Big Man'

From a seedling of *M.* 'Giganteus' and similar to it in most respects but smaller. Propagate by division. Zone 5.

Miscanthus 'Purpurascens'

This cultivar usually has the most reliable red-or-ange fall foliage color of any miscanthus grown in the United States, an attribute combined with small size, upright stature, early flowering, and extreme cold hardiness to make this a superb choice. It does not belong to *M. sinensis*, and is possibly a hybrid involving *M. oligostachyus*, but its ultimate origin is obscure. It was selected in the 1960s by Hans Simon of Germany, from seed obtained from Japan. Ironically, the fall color is not reliable in Germany and the plant is not widely grown there. It colors well but often does not flower in England. Blooms in warm climates in late July or August, to 5 ft. (1.5 m), the inflorescences narrow and vertical, with few raceme branches, opening with slight pink tints and drying silvery. Leaves to $^1/2$ in. (12 mm) wide, slightly gray-green in summer. Never needs staking and performs satisfactorily even in light shade, in which case the fall foliage colors are various pas-

Miscanthus sacchariflorus in Pennsylvania in late August.

Miscanthus sacchariflorus 'Gotemba' in Pennsylvania in early September.

tels. Not drought tolerant, suffers in extreme heat. Because it rarely if ever self-sows, it is one of the best choices for gardens adjacent to natural areas in the eastern United States. Zone 4.

Miscanthus sacchariflorus
Silver banner grass

Native and common to wet lowlands of Japan. Also native to Manchuria, Ussuri, Korea, and northern China. Primarily distinguished by its stout rhizomes, strongly running habit, and the lack of awns in the flower spikelets. Blooms in August, to 8 ft. (2.4 m) tall, the flowers held well above the foliage, opening silver and becoming fluffy-white upon drying. The inflorescences are narrower and more upright than those of *M. sinensis* and remain attractive through most of winter. Leaves to $1^1/4$ in. (32 mm) wide, with pronounced white midrib, turning yellow in autumn. Often loses lower foliage during summer dry periods. The spreading habit is useful for colonizing large sites, such as

parking lot berms or banks of ponds, but can be difficult to control in smaller gardens. Spreads more slowly on heavy soils. Self-sows prolifically and has proved to be a serious invasive in parts of the upper Midwest. Zone 4.

'Gotemba'. Dramatic bright yellow and green-striped foliage. From Japan's Gotemba nursery. An exceptionally aggressive runner best contained. Zone 6.

'Robustus'. Supposedly larger than the type but usually indistinguishable. Zone 4.

Miscanthus sinensis
Eulalia, Japanese silver grass

Native to slopes in the lowlands and mountains of Japan, Yaku Island, the Ryukyus to Taiwan, southern Kuriles, Korea, and China. This is the premier *Miscanthus* species, of exceptional beauty and variability, but always strictly clump-forming. The typical form is rarely grown, having medium-green leaves to $3/4$ in. (2 cm) wide with prominent white midrib. Produced from August to October, the inflorescences are full and dense, each with numerous racemes, opening reddish and fading to silver-white upon drying. Typical fall foliage color is yellow.

The myriad cultivated varieties differ significantly in size, height, texture, summer and autumn foliage color, flowering times and colors, and cold hardiness. A sampling of the best or most widely available follows. All prefer full sun unless otherwise noted. Heights are for mature specimens under best conditions; many grow much smaller in colder or drier conditions. Hardiness zones listed are based on observed performance; some cultivars may prove more cold hardy with further evaluation. Unless otherwise stated, all are propagated by division.

'Adagio'. A diminutive selection, similar to 'Yaku Jima', but superior for its consistent production of inflorescences that extend beyond the tops of the foliage. Leaves green, very narrow, turning yellow in autumn. Blooms in August, to 5 ft. (1.5 m). Inflorescences open with red tints. A good fine-textured choice for smaller gardens. Zone 6.

Miscanthus sinensis 'Adagio' in early October in Maryland.

Miscanthus sinensis 'Ferner Osten' in late August in Germany.

Miscanthus sinensis 'Goldfeder' foliage in late August in Pennsylvania.

Miscanthus sinensis 'Gracillimus' in late February, after winter storms have reduced the inflorescence to a stunning filigree.

The rounded form of *Miscanthus sinensis* 'Gracillimus' has made it a favorite of gardeners since Victorian days.

Miscanthus sinensis 'Graziella' in Maryland in early November.

Plumes of *Miscanthus sinensis* 'Malepartus' are snowy white in early October in Maryland.

Miscanthus sinensis 'Hinjo' in Pennsylvania in mid-August.

'**Autumn Light**'. Tall, to 8 ft. (2.4 m), with green, narrow leaves. Blooms in September. Zone 5.

'**Dixieland**'. Similar to 'Variegatus' but more compact. Zone 6.

'**Ferner Osten**' ('Far East'). Inflorescences with a very pronounced red color when first opening in mid to late summer. Slightly wider leaves and earlier blooming than 'Gracillimus'. Zone 6, likely colder.

'**Flamingo**'. Large, loosely open, pink-tinted inflorescences with relatively few raceme branches, which are slightly pendent. Blooms late summer, to 6 ft. (2 m). Zone 5.

'**Goldfeder**' ('Gold Feather'). One of the most distinct and beautiful variegated miscanthus, with leaves to $^3/_4$ in. (2 cm) wide, longitudinally striped light golden yellow. Little known only because it is slow to propagate and has been somewhat difficult to obtain commercially. Discovered in the late 1950s as a sport on 'Silberfeder' and similar to it in being somewhat open growing, with midsummer inflorescences held well above the foliage, opening silver, not red-tinted. To 7 ft. (2.1 m) tall. The variegation darkens to light yellow-green by late summer. Zone 6.

'**Gracillimus**'. Maiden grass. One of the oldest and perhaps the best-known *Miscanthus* cultivars, valued for its foliage and gracefully rounded overall form. The fine texture of this large grass demonstrates that size and texture can be independent of one another. 'Gracillimus' is among the last to bloom, the copper-red inflorescences opening in late September or October, or not at all in regions with short growing seasons. To 7 ft. (2.1 m) tall in bloom. Fall foliage color golden yellow. This cultivar has been propagated by seed and division over the decades. Plants purchased as 'Gracillimus' should have narrow leaves, rounded form, and late-season reddish flowers, but they may not all be identical. Mature specimens tend to flop, especially if at all shaded, too moist, or fertility is high. Though many earlier-blooming, green, narrow-leaved alternatives to 'Gracillimus' are now available, not all possess the graceful rounded form. Three that come close are 'Ferner Osten', 'Graziella', and 'Silberspinne'. Zone 5.

'**Graziella**'. Leaves narrow, green. Blooms in August or early September, the inflorescences opening mostly silver, held high above the foliage, very fluffy when dry, to 7 ft. (2.1 m) tall. Slightly more upright in form than 'Gracillimus'. Fall foliage color usually rich copper red and orange. Very beautiful and refined. Zone 5.

'**Grosse Fontäne**' ('Large Fountain'). Leaves green, midsummer flowers, to 8 ft. (2.4 m). Zone 5.

'**Hinjo**' (Little Nicky™). A superb cultivar with much of the character of 'Zebrinus' but significantly smaller in all aspects, to 6 ft. (2 m) in full flower, and never flops. The horizontal bands of yellow variegation are quite vivid and are more closely spaced than those of 'Zebrinus' or 'Strictus', making a stronger impression, especially from a distance. The best choice in banded-leaved miscanthus for smaller gardens. Zone 5.

'**Juli**' ('July'). Broad green leaves, early summer flowering. Upright and somewhat coarse-textured. Few branches to the inflorescence, an indication that this is a likely hybrid involving *M. oligostachyus*. Zone 6.

'**Kascade**' ('Cascade'). Named for the large, loosely open, pink-tinted inflorescences, which have relatively few, slightly pendent raceme branches. Blooms midsummer, to 7 ft. (2.1 m). Upright and slightly narrow in form, with flowers held high above the foliage. Zone 5.

'**Kirk Alexander**'. Leaves with horizontal bands of yellow variegation. Free-flowering and more compact than 'Zebrinus', but leaf banding not nearly as vivid as 'Hinjo'. Named for landscape architect Kirk Alexander. Zone 6.

'**Kleine Fontäne**' ('Little Fountain'). Similar to 'Grosse Fontäne' but smaller. Zone 5.

'**Little Kitten**'. Narrow-leaved and extremely compact, under 3 ft. (1 m) tall in flower. Originated as a seedling from 'Yaku Jima'. Leaves green, flowers sparsely. Zone 6.

'**Malepartus**'. Blooms early September. Leaves wider than those of 'Graziella' but similar in form. Flowers open silver, become very fluffy-white when dry, to 7 ft. (2.1 m) tall. Fall foliage color gold, often with strong infusions of orange and red. Zone 5.

'Morning Light'. Arguably the best all-around garden plant among the *Miscanthus* species and cultivars. It has the narrow foliage, fine texture, and rounded form of 'Gracillimus', with leaf margins cleanly and uniformly white-variegated. Blooms late, with reddish flowers and is not inclined to self-sowing, although it may do so in warm, moist parts of the southeastern United States. Unlike 'Gracillimus', it never flops. Known to cultivation in Japan for at least a century, but first introduced to Western gardens in 1976. Of great refinement and elegance, this versatile selection is especially beautiful near water or grown in a container. Tolerates light shade. To 6 ft. (2 m) in flower. Zone 5.

'Puenktchen' ('Little Dot'). Has banded variegation similar to 'Strictus' with leaves even more stiffly held. Very spiky texture. Zone 5.

'Rigoletto'. Similar to 'Variegatus' but more compact. Zone 6.

'Sarabande'. Similar to 'Gracillimus' but narrower leaves and finer textured overall. Golden copper inflorescences in August, to 6 ft. (2 m). Zone 5.

'Silberfeder' ('Silver Feather'). Large feathery flowers emerge silver with only the slightest pink tint. Leaves green, $^3/_4$ in. (2 cm) wide. Inflorescences held very high above the foliage, to 7 ft. (2.1 m), appearing in August. Stems often slightly lax and may flop even in sun, but do this gracefully. Free-flowering, even in England, where it has long been a favorite. Zone 4.

'Silberspinne' ('Silver Spider'). Narrow green leaves, upright form, flowers opening silver with pink tints in midsummer, to 6 ft. (2 m). Particularly graceful. Zone 5.

'Strictus' ('Zebrinus Strictus'). Porcupine grass. Known in Western gardens for a century. Similiar to 'Zebrinus' but significantly more upright in stature and less inclined to flop. Leaves are held more erect, like porcupine quills, increasing the effectiveness of the variegation and making for an overall more spiky effect. Blooms in September, opening reddish, to 9 ft. (2.7 m). Zone 5.

'Variegatus'. The white-striped foliage of this antique cultivar still provides the strongest white

Miscanthus sinensis 'Morning Light' foliage in mid-July in the author's former Delaware garden.

A dark ornamental pool mirrors the beauty of a superbly placed specimen of *Miscanthus sinensis* 'Morning Light' in New York in mid-September.

Miscanthus sinensis 'Silberfeder' in mid-September in Delaware.

The quill-like leaves of porcupine grass, Miscanthus sinensis 'Strictus', project at sharp angles in two plants growing side by side in Pennsylvania in mid-September.

Miscanthus sinensis 'Variegatus' in early July in England.

Miscanthus sinensis 'Yaku Jima' and *Panicum virgatum* 'Heavy Metal' (at left) in late September in Pennsylvania.

Miscanthus sinensis 'Zebrinus' foliage in late July in Pennsylvania.

landscape effect of all the miscanthus; unfortunately mature specimens usually need staking. Blooms in mid-September, opening strongly red-tinted, to 7 ft. (2.1 m). Young plants make superb container specimens. Zone 5.

'Yaku Jima'. Not a clonal cultivar, but a name used for several very similar, compact, narrow-leaved plants, usually less than 5 ft. (1.5 m) tall. Diminutive forms of *M. sinensis* are common on the Japanese island of Yaku. Staff of the U.S. National Arboretum, Washington, D.C., first brought 'Yaku Jima' seedlings to the United States that were variable but similar in being small and narrow-leaved. The name 'Yaku Jima' has been used by nurseries as a catch-all for these seedlings and their progeny. Zone 6.

'Zebrinus'. Zebra grass. The lax green leaves have irregularly spaced horizontal bands of yellow variegation. Flowers copper tinted in mid-September, to 8 ft. (2.4 m). Although the foliage is more graceful and the overall effect less formal than that of 'Strictus', this venerable old cultivar

usually requires staking. It has been surpassed by the more compact 'Hinjo'. Zone 5.

Miscanthus sinensis var. *condensatus*
Hachijo susuki

This botanical variety most frequently grows in coastal areas of Japan, in vast sweeps reminiscent of *Phragmites australis* masses growing in similar cultural conditions in eastern North America and on other continents. Var. *condensatus* is also found at higher elevations in Japan as well as in Korea, China, Indochina, and the Pacific islands. It has been recognized as a separate species by some taxonomists. It is not a cultivar, although it is sometimes incorrectly labeled 'Condensatus'. Stouter, more robust, and wider-leaved than the typical species, this variety usually produces an extra flush of growth late in autumn, and the foliage remains green longer in winter. Blooms in late summer, opening red-copper tinted. Fall color is yellow and not significant; however, the two following cultivars have the most dramatically variegated summer foliage of all the miscanthus. Good near water. Zone 5.

'Cabaret'. This is the boldest and most spectacular of all the variegated miscanthus. To 1 1/4 in. (32 mm) wide, the leaves are cream-white in the center with wide dark green margins. 'Cabaret' requires a long warm season for

Literally millions of *Miscanthus sinensis* var. *condensatus* grow in a moist, sunny native habitat in Japan's coastal lowlands, catching the morning light in late October.

Miscanthus sinensis var. *condensatus* 'Cabaret' foliage in late September.

flowering, but is worth growing just for the foliage. Cut stems make stunning additions to fresh bouquets. Blooms in late September, mature specimens to 9 ft. (2.7 m). Flowering stems are often suffused deep pink in late summer and autumn. Sturdy and upright, rarely requiring staking or support. Individual stems occasionally revert to solid green and should be removed. Tony Avent of Plant Delights Nursery has found that 'Cabaret' is seed-sterile. Germinating seedlings routinely lack chlorophyll and do not survive. A superb container subject. Tolerates light shade. Propagate by division. Zone 6.

'Cosmopolitan'. Leaves to $1^1/_2$ in. (4 cm) wide, with mostly green centers and wide cream-white variegated margins, in a pattern nearly the reverse of 'Cabaret'. 'Cosmopolitan' flowers much more freely and slightly earlier than 'Cabaret', opening copper-red in early September, to 10 ft. (3 m). Individual stems occasionally revert to solid green and should be removed. Originally found in Japan in the 1940s by Toyoichi Aoki of Tokyo. A superb container subject. Tolerates light shade. Propagate by division. Zone 6.

'Cosmo Revert'. All-green plants segregated from 'Cosmopolitan'.

Miscanthus sinensis var. *condensatus* 'Cosmopolitan' flowering in late September in Pennsylvania.

Miscanthus transmorrisonensis flowering in mid-July in North Carolina.

Miscanthus sinensis foliage in late September from plants growing in Pennsylvania (from top): var. *condensatus* 'Cosmopolitan'; var. *condensatus* 'Cabaret'; 'Variegatus'; 'Goldfeder'; 'Morning Light'; 'Gracillimus'; *M. sinensis* (typical species form); 'Strictus'.

Miscanthus transmorrisonensis
Taiwanese miscanthus

An introduction from Taiwan from seed collected from plants growing at 9500 ft. (2900 m) elevation on Mount Daxue. This species is frequent on exposed mountain slopes at medium to high altitudes throughout Taiwan. It is closely related to *M. sinensis* but horticulturally quite distinct, with narrow green foliage rarely topping 3 ft. (1 m) and late July or early August flowers held high above the foliage on long graceful stems. The foliage often stays green into late December as far north as zone 6 and is fully evergreen in southern California. A beautiful, distinct miscanthus. Propagate by seed or division. Zone 6.

MOLINIA
Moor grass (Grass family)

Named for Juan I. Molina (1740–1829), who studied the natural history of Chile. Comprised of two or three clump-forming perennial species, native to wet moorlands and heaths in Europe, western Russia, Turkey, China, and Japan. Only *M. caerulea* is grown for ornament, and it is usually separated into two subspecies, which differ dramatically in height and other less obvious characters. Subsp. *caerulea* usually grows less than 3 ft. (1 m) tall and is called purple moor grass, whereas subsp. *arundinacea* grows to 8 ft. (2.4 m) and is called tall purple moor grass. One cultivar with variegated leaves is prized for its foliage; the other cultivars are essentially green plants valued for their strong architectural forms and airy inflorescences. They are cool-season growers that grow best in moist, cool climates.

Molinia caerulea
Purple moor grass

Native to heaths, moors, bogs, fens, mountain grasslands, and lake shores in the British Isles as well as continental Europe and Asia. Strictly clumping, producing a low mound of basal foliage, with leaves to $3/8$ in. (9 mm) wide, usually green, typically turning golden yellow in autumn. Blooms in midsummer, the narrow panicles held above the foliage on slender stalks varying from strictly upright to strongly arched, to 3 ft. (1 m) tall. Flower spikelets are purple, but this color is subtle due to their small size. Requires moist, cool summer conditions for best growth. Flowering is minimal in regions with hot summers, especially if conditions are dry. Partly shaded conditions and plentiful moisture can help to offset heat stress. Tolerates low soil fertility and acid conditions, but also grows on alkaline soils common to the north-central United States. Propagate the species by seed or by division in spring, the cultivars only by division. Zone 4.

'**Dauerstrahl**' ('Faithful Ray'). Green-leaved and arching. Zone 4.

'**Heidebraut**' ('Heather Bride'). Green-leaved and upright-divergent. Zone 4.

'**Moorhexe**' ('Moor Witch'). Green-leaved and narrowly erect. Zone 4.

Molinia caerulea 'Dauerstrahl' in late August in northern Germany.

Molinia caerulea 'Heidebraut' in late August in northern Germany.

Molinia caerulea 'Moorhexe' in late August in northern Germany.

Molinia caerulea 'Strahlenquelle' in late August in Germany.

Molinia caerulea 'Variegata' in late August in northern Germany.

'Strahlenquelle' ('Source of Rays'). Green-leaved with strongly arching-pendant inflorescences that are bowed under the weight of the delicate purplish flowers. Zone 4.

'Variegata'. Leaves dramatically striped light yellow to cream-white. In regions where flowering is heavy, the bright yellow stalks of the inflorescences are attractive, but this plant is worth growing just for the foliage. Zone 5.

Molinia caerulea subsp. *arundinacea*
Tall purple moor grass

Differs from the typical subspecies dramatically in height and other less obvious characters: subspecies *caerulea* usually grows less than 3 ft. (1 m) tall, whereas subspecies *arundinacea* grows to 8 ft. (2.4 m) tall. Native to fens, fen scrub, and along rivers in the British Isles as well as to continental Europe and Asia. Produces mounded basal foliage 2–3 ft. (60–90 cm) tall, topped by stately inflorescences to 8 ft. (2.4 m) tall, either upright or arching. Leaves green or gray-green in summer, to $^{1}/_{2}$ in. (12 mm) wide. The entire plant turns rich golden yellow in autumn. The appeal of this large grass is in its strong sculptural form

Molinia caerulea subsp. *arundinacea* 'Karl Foerster' in early September in Washington, D.C.

Molinia caerulea subsp. *arundinacea* 'Transparent' in mid-August in southern Germany.

Molinia caerulea subsp. *arundinacea* 'Skyracer' in early November in Pennsylvania.

and in the graceful way the inflorescences move with the wind. Most effective when side-lit or back-lit by the sun, especially against a contrasting background. Needs a few seasons to reach mature size and beauty, but will last for many years with minimal maintenance. Best in cool climates, but grows strongly even in areas with fairly hot summers as long as it is kept moist. Not particular about soils. Tolerates low soil fertility and acid conditions, but also grows on alkaline soils common to the north-central United States. The flower stalks begin to break off at the ground by early winter, at which time the plant is best cut back. Propagate the subspecies by seed or by division in spring, the cultivars only by division. Zone 4.

'**Bergfreund**' ('Mountain Friend'). To 5 ft. (1.5 m). Zone 4.

'**Fontäne**' ('Fountain'). Arching form, to 6 ft. (2 m). Zone 4.

'**Karl Foerster**'. Arching form, to 7 ft. (2.1 m). Named for the famous German nurseryman and ornamental grass pioneer. Zone 4.

'**Skyracer**'. Upright and unusually tall, to 8 ft. (2.4 m). Zone 4.

'Staefa'. Mostly upright, to 5 ft. (1.5 m). Named for the Swiss city. Zone 4.

'Transparent'. Arching form, to 6 ft. (2 m). The name refers to the transparent section between the top of the basal foliage and the point on the inflorescence stalks where the flowers begin. Zone 4.

'Windspiel' ('Wind's Game'). Slender and upright, to 7 ft. (2.1 m). The name alludes to the wind playing with the supple and responsive inflorescences. Zone 4.

MUHLENBERGIA
Muhly (Grass family)

Named for botanist G. H. E. Muhlenberg (1753–1815), a specialist in grasses. Comprised of approximately 125 primarily perennial species, most native to the southern United States and Mexico. They are important range grasses, forming a large portion of the grass flora of semi-arid and arid regions in the Southwest. Tolerant to sun and drought, many muhly grasses have attractive, fine-textured green to glaucous blue basal foliage topped by airy inflorescences, some of which are strongly colored pink, purple-red, or purple-gray. Little known to ornamental horticulture, these species are increasingly attracting attention as water-conserving ornamentals for hot, dry regions. A few species are wide-ranging, and provenance will likely prove an important factor in selecting plants with greater cold hardiness for garden use.

Muhlenbergia capillaris
Pink muhly, pink hair grass

Native mostly on sandy or rocky soils, in prairies, pine barrens, and openings in woodlands from Massachusetts to Indiana and Kansas south to Florida, Texas, and Mexico. Plants of moist coastal barrens are considered here to be synonymous with *M. capillaris*. The most highly ornamental of the muhly grasses, with dark green, glossy basal foliage overtopped by masses of delicate open flower panicles in vibrant pink or pink-red, drying to light buff. Blooms September to November, to

A sweep of *Muhlenbergia capillaris* forms a vibrant pink-red mass in early October in North Carolina.

3 ft. (1 m) tall, remaining attractive into winter. Clump-forming. Effective singly, but especially dramatic in groups and sweeps. Tough enough for groundcover use and in challenging settings, such as traffic islands, even in the warm southeastern United States. Drought tolerant, best in full sun or very light shade. Propagate by seed or by division in spring. Zone 6, if soggy winter soil conditions are avoided.

Muhlenbergia dubia
Pine muhly

Native to canyons and rocky hills at elevations to 7000 ft. (2100 m) in western Texas, New Mexico, and northern Mexico. Clump-forming and densely tufted with light green, fine-textured leaves. Blooms August to November, the inflorescences stiff, narrow, purplish gray fading quickly to light cream color, 2–3 ft. (60–90 cm) tall. Drought tolerant. Prefers full sun. Propagate by seed or by division in spring. Zone 7.

Muhlenbergia dumosa
Bamboo muhly

Native to rocky canyon slopes and valleys at low elevations in southern Arizona and northwestern Mexico. Very distinct from the other muhly grasses, with billowing, lacy, bright green foliage and leafy, erect or arching stems to 4 ft. (1.2 m) that move gracefully with the slightest breeze.

Muhlenbergia dubia in mid-November in Texas.

Muhlenbergia dumosa in a decorative container in mid-September in Pennsylvania.

Muhlenbergia dumosa foliage detail.

The overall effect is quite like bamboo. Spreads slowly by creeping rhizomes. Blooms March to May, flowers insignificant. Drought tolerant, but not as much as other *Muhlenbergia* species; best with occasional moisture. A fine companion for cacti and other bold-textured succulents. Makes a superb container specimen or conservatory subject in areas where it is not cold hardy. Propagate by seed or division. Zone 8, possibly colder.

Muhlenbergia emersleyi
Bull grass

Native to rocky slopes, woods, canyons, and ravines in Arizona, New Mexico, and Texas. Clump-forming with medium-textured gray-green leaves in a dense basal mound. Blooms August to November, the inflorescences mostly erect, to 3 ft. (1 m), purplish gray, dense, not airy like *M. capillaris*. Drought tolerant. Best in full sun or light shade. Propagate by seed or division. Zone 7, possibly colder.

Muhlenbergia lindheimeri
Lindheimer's muhly

Native to Mexico and Texas. A stunning clump-former with fine-textured, semi-evergreen blue-gray basal leaves. Inflorescences upright, to 5 ft. (1.5 m) tall, vaguely reminiscent of *Calamagrostis*. Drought tolerant and summer-heat tolerant, does well even in the southeastern United States. Blooms September to October, the inflorescences light purplish gray, lasting through most of winter. Prefers full sun. Propagate by seed or division. Zone 7, possibly colder.

Autumn Glow™. A clonal selection made by Mountain States Nursery of Arizona. Inflorescences yellowish in autumn.

Muhlenbergia reverchonii
Seep muhly

Native to limestone soils and periodic seep areas in Texas and Oklahoma. Clump-forming and

The graceful flowering stems of *Muhlenbergia lindheimeri* are set off dramatically by the autumn red of sumac in mid-October in the author's Pennsylvania garden.

Long before flowering begins, the mounded blue-gray basal foliage of *Muhlenbergia lindheimeri* is attractive in this North Carolina garden in mid-July.

Muhlenbergia reverchonii in mid-November in Texas.

Muhlenbergia rigens and California poppies in late May in California.

Muhlenbergia rigens is side-lit by the late February sun against native live oaks in this ruggedly beautiful California landscape.

densely tufted with green leaves. Blooms August to October, the inflorescences to 2^{1}/2 ft. (80 cm) tall, open and airy. Propagate by seed or division. Zone 6, possibly colder.

Muhlenbergia rigens
Deer grass

Native to dry or open ground, hillsides, gullies, and open forest to 7000 ft. (2100 m) elevation in California, Arizona, Nevada, New Mexico, Texas, and southern Mexico. Clump-forming with gray-green leaves forming a large basal mound, semi-evergreen. Blooms in late summer, the inflorescences narrow, whiplike, to 5 ft. (1.5 m), soon drying to a light straw color, remaining upright and attractive long through winter. A stunning vertical accent, especially when side-lit or back-lit by the autumn or winter sun. Very drought tolerant. Prefers full sun. Propagate by seed or division. Zone 7, possibly colder.

NASSELLA
Needle grass (Grass family)

Comprised of approximately 80 species native to the Americas. Many, including those below, were formerly included in *Stipa*. All are graceful, cool-season growers with long, showy awns.

Nassella cernua
Nodding needle grass

Native to sandy, dry slopes in grasslands, chaparral, and juniper woodlands in California. Clump-forming and tufted. A true cool-season grower, dormant in summer. Blooms in late winter to early spring, inflorescences delicate and open, to 3 ft. (1 m), with awns to 4^{1}/2 in. (11 cm) long, purplish at first, drying silvery, usually nodding. Similar in appearance to *N. lepida* and *N. pulchra*, and all were once a conspicuous part of California native grasslands. Prefers full sun, best on well-drained soil but broadly tolerant. Ideal for naturalizing in meadows and meadow gardens, but needs open ground for seeds to establish.

Nassella cernua is backed by native shrubby *Arctostaphylos* in mid-June in California.

Self-sows but not invasive. Propagate by seed. Zone 8.

Nassella lepida
Foothill needle grass
Native to dry slopes in oak grasslands, chaparral, and coastal scrub in California. Clump-forming and tufted. A true cool-season grower, dormant in summer. Blooms in late winter or early spring, inflorescences delicate and open, with awns nearly 2 in. (5 cm) long. Prefers full sun, best on well-drained soil but broadly tolerant. Ideal for naturalizing in meadows and meadow gardens, but needs open ground for seeds to establish. Self-sows but not invasive. Propagate by seed. Zone 8.

Nassella pulchra
Purple needle grass
Native to dry grasslands, chaparral, and coastal scrub in California. Delicately beautiful; an emblem of the dry native grasslands that once covered much of California. Blooms in late winter or early spring. Inflorescences on erect stalks, to 3 ft. (1 m) tall. Spikelets with graceful long awns, to 4 in. (10 cm), purple at first, turning silvery and translucent. A cool-season grower, dormant in summer, resuming growth in fall and usually green through winter. Prefers full sun, best on well-drained soil but broadly tolerant. Ideal for naturalizing in meadows and meadow gardens, but needs open ground for seeds to establish. Self-sows but not invasive. Propagate by seed. Zone 8.

Nassella tenuissima
Mexican feather grass
Native to dry open ground, open woods, and rocky slopes in Texas, New Mexico, Mexico, and Argentina. Among the finest-textured ornamental grasses, producing a dense green fountain of hairlike leaves and threadlike stems ending in silvery inflorescences with awns more than 3 in. (7.5 cm) long. Blooms June to September, to 2 ft. (60 cm) tall, the inflorescences becoming a

Nassella tenuissima in mid-July in England.

light straw color and remaining attractive into winter. Stunning in contrast to rocks or bold-textured companion plantings. Delicate and easily moved by breezes. Easily grown on well-drained soil in full sun or light shade. Very drought tolerant. A cool-season grower that remains evergreen in cool climates but goes dormant during hot summers. Self-sows readily and can be a minor nuisance. May be capable of naturalizing in areas, such as California and the Pacific Northwest. Propagate by seed. Zone 6, if soggy winter soil conditions are avoided.

PANICUM
Panic grass, switchgrass (Grass family)

Includes nearly 500 annual and perennial species native to deserts, savannas, swamps, and forests, widely distributed in tropical regions, and extending to temperate North America. The inflorescences are panicles with narrow or more often wide-spreading branches. The following species are increasingly important ornamentally, due in large part to the development of distinctly beautiful cultivated varieties. Seedling plants from clonal cultivars of both *Panicum* species often vary considerably from the parent. Both species are among the larger switchgrasses and can be used as specimens, to organize garden spaces, or to create deciduous screening. As such, both offer attractive alternatives to *Miscanthus* in the garden.

Nassella pulchra in late February with California poppies, *Eschscholzia californica*, in California.

Panicum amarum
Bitter switchgrass, coastal switchgrass

This species grows naturally only on sandy soils along the North American coast from New Jersey south to Florida and Texas. The inflorescences are much narrower and less plumelike than *P. virgatum*, and the foliage is more often glaucous, with an overall gray-green or blue-green appearance. It also increases more rapidly by rhizomes. Leaves typically $^{1}/_{2}$ in. (12 mm) wide. Mature plants grow 3–6 ft. (90–180 cm) tall. Valued for its role in coastal soil stabilization, this species has real potential as an ornamental in full-sun garden settings, especially where soils are relatively low in fertility and summers are dry. It has also proved adapted to soggy soils. Propagates readily by seed or division. Zone 6.

'Dewey Blue'. Leaves especially gray-blue. Selected from plants grown from seed of a native population along the coast in Dewey, Delaware. Blooms late July or early August. In rich soil 5 ft. (1.5 m) tall, much shorter in sand. Zone 6, likely colder.

Panicum amarum growing naturally in sandy soil in Delaware in early August.

The gray-blue color of *Panicum amarum* 'Dewey Blue' is particularly strong in morning light in the author's Pennsylvania garden in early August.

Panicum virgatum in early July in native habitat of coastal New Jersey.

Panicum virgatum glows gold in mid-October in native habitat of coastal New Jersey.

Panicum virgatum growth from the previous season is still attractive in mid-May, at water's edge, with *Orontium aquaticum* in the New Jersey pine barrens.

The flowers of *Panicum virgatum* 'Dallas Blues' are light pink in mid-September in Pennsylvania.

Panicum virgatum
Common switchgrass

Native to prairies and open ground, open woods, and brackish marshes from eastern Canada through most of the United States, except California and the Pacific Northwest, south to Mexico and Central America. Once a major component of the great American tallgrass prairie. Diverse in size, growing 4–8 ft. (1.2–2.4 m) tall. Always forms recognizable clumps but may also run (slowly or moderately) by rhizomes. It may be erect and narrow, or lax and billowing in form. Summer foliage color ranges from typical deep green to bright powder-blue, and autumn tones vary from typical golden yellow to deep burgundy. A long-lived, warm-season grower, it begins growth late in spring, grows strongly in the heat of summer, and flowers in July or August. The profuse, airy panicles are often pink or red-tinted when first opening.

All parts of the plant are sturdy even when dry and dormant, standing through winter unless snows are heavy, and providing important cover for birds. Effective as a specimen, in sweeps or masses, for screening, at the edges of pools or ponds, or in large decorative containers. Of easy culture in full sun on almost any soil . Drought tolerant once established, yet withstands soggy soils or periodic inundation. Self-sowing is usually minimal but can be prolific on open moist soil. Requires little maintenance except cutting back annually in late winter or early spring. The extremely blue-leaved cultivars generally do not have the strong golden autumn color typical of green-leaved plants, and none turn red in fall. Propagate the species by seed or by division in spring, the cultivars by division only. Zone 4.

'Blue Tower'. Tall blue switchgrass. Leaves glaucous-blue, to 8 ft. (2.4 m) tall in flower. A selection from a native population in Princeton, Illinois. Zone 4.

'Campfire'. Red switchgrass. Smaller than average, similar in size to 'Shenandoah'. Autumn foliage colors are a vibrant mix of rich red and orange.

'Cloud Nine'. Tall switchgrass. Leaves glaucous blue-green, to 8 ft. (2.4 m) tall in flower, erect, and usually upright through winter, a pleasing dark gold in autumn. Zone 4.

Panicum virgatum 'Cloud Nine' in mid-September in Pennsylvania.

Panicum virgatum 'Dallas Blues' flowers have deepened to a lavender-purple hue by late September in the author's Pennsylvania garden.

Panicum virgatum 'Dallas Blues' flower panicles are deep purple-red, rivaling the best miscanthus, in mid-October in Pennsylvania.

Panicum virgatum 'Dallas Blues' is tawny and luminous in mid-November sunlight in the author's Pennsylvania garden.

Panicum virgatum 'Hänse Herms' makes a fine container specimen next to threadleaf bluestar, *Amsonia hubrichtii*, in mid-October in Pennsylvania.

Panicum virgatum 'Northwind' in mid-September in Pennsylvania.

Panicum virgatum 'Heavy Metal' (two clumps, front left) is strictly upright, whereas *P. virgatum* 'Hänse Herms' (front right) is lax-stemmed and arching in early August, after a moist season, in Pennsylvania.

Panicum virgatum 'Prairie Sky' foliage is strongly gray-blue in late June in Pennsylvania.

The vertical stance of *Panicum virgatum* 'Northwind' is dramatically apparent in this mid-July planting in the author's Pennsylvania garden.

In late September, a production block at a Maryland nursery demonstrates the impact of a sweep of *Panicum virgatum* 'Shenandoah'.

Panicum virgatum 'Shenandoah' foliage is mostly burgundy in late September in the author's Pennsylvania garden.

'**Dallas Blues**'. A distinct and outstanding new introduction with broad, steel-blue to gray-green foliage and dramatic purplish flower panicles. Selected from seedlings growing in a Dallas, Texas, garden. Big and bold-textured, reaching 6–7 ft. (1.8–2.1 m) height with leaves ³/₄–1¹/₂ in. (2–4 cm) wide. It flowers later than most of the other cultivars, usually beginning bloom in mid to late September. The sturdy stems and inflorescences stand up well into winter. Prefers full sun. Higher than average drought tolerance. Zone 4.

'**Hänse Herms**'. Red switchgrass. Leaves green in summer, taking on dark red tones by August, and turning mostly burgundy in autumn. Among the best for this trait. Just over 4 ft. (1.2 m) in flower. Stems bend gracefully during rains, usually returning to upright position upon drying, but may lodge permanently after prolonged rainy periods. Zone 4.

'**Heavy Metal**'. Blue switchgrass. Leaves strongly glaucous-blue and strictly upright. Stems never lean or flop, even in heavy rains. To 5 ft. (1.5 m) tall in bloom, with strong pink tones in the inflorescences. Prone to foliar rust diseases in hot, moist summers. Zone 4.

'Northwind'. Similar in size and foliage color to 'Cloud Nine', but much narrower in form, remaining upright through autumn and most of winter. Among the most drought tolerant of *P. virgatum* cultivars, with thicker, heavier leaves that resist rolling even in very dry periods. Zone 4.

'Prairie Sky'. Blue switchgrass. Leaves noticeably bluer than that of 'Heavy Metal'. Not as sturdy-stemmed and sometimes flops in wet seasons common to the eastern United States. Stands upright in drier, western regions. Zone 4.

'Red Cloud'. Red switchgrass. Leaves green in summer, purplish in autumn. Flowers strongly red tinted, to 5^1/$_2$ ft. (1.7 m) tall. Zone 4.

'Rotbraun' ('Red-Brown'). Red switchgrass. Similar to 'Hänse Herms', but the autumn burgundy-red tones are not as pronounced. To 4 ft. (1.2 m) tall in flower. Zone 4.

'Rotstrahlbusch'. Red switchgrass. Leaves red-burgundy in autumn, but not nearly as pronounced as 'Hänse Herms'. To 4 ft. (1.2 m) tall. Zone 4.

'Shenandoah'. Red switchgrass. Unmatched for dark burgundy fall color. Leaves green in early summer, taking on dark red tones by July and turning wholly wine-colored by September. Approximately 4 ft. (1.2 m) tall in flower, and among the lowest, slowest growing switchgrass cultivars currently available. Selected by Hans Simon of Germany, from his evaluations of more than 500 seedlings of 'Hänse Herms'. Zone 4.

'Squaw'. Leaves green, to 4 ft. (1.2 m) in flower. The flower panicles are noticeably pink to red in late summer. Zone 4.

'Strictum'. Leaves blue-green, to 6 ft. (2 m) in flower. Zone 4.

'Warrior'. Leaves green, to 5 ft. (1.5 m) in flower. The flower panicles are noticeably pink to red in late summer. Zone 4.

PENNISETUM
Fountain grass (Grass family)

The genus name means "feather bristle," referring to the bristlelike inflorescences. Comprised of approximately 80 species, mostly perennials, native to both open and woodland habitats,

Pennisetum alopecuroides foliage in late June in Pennsylvania.

widely distributed in the tropics and in warm temperate regions. These grasses are characterized by a fountain of flowers flowing out of a cascading mound of basal foliage. They are warm-season growers, unperturbed by hot, humid summers, flowering from late June to October. Most are clump-forming, though a few are strong runners. Most prefer full sun or light shade and are best divided or transplanted in spring. Many self-sow readily, and a few have escaped from cultivation to become serious weeds in warm regions, such as southern Cali-

fornia and Australia. Particularly in California, the native *Calamgrostis* species offer attractive alternatives. Though the following *Pennisetum* species are true perennials, a few are tender tropicals that are grown as annuals in cold-temperate regions.

Pennisetum alopecuroides
Fountain grass, chikara shiba

Native to sunny open lowlands and grassy places in Japan and much of eastern Asia. Of uncertain nativity in western Australia. This extremely

Pennisetum alopecuroides blooms in late July in North Carolina.

Pennisetum alopecuroides foliage takes on rich golden autumn tones in Pennsylvania in mid-October.

Pennisetum alopecuroides is beautifully frosted in late October in southeastern Pennsylvania, in combination with *Sedum* 'Autumn Joy', *Rudbeckia* 'Goldsturm', and *Cornus florida*.

Pennisetum alopecuroides 'Hameln' in early August in Pennsylvania.

variable species is the most commonly grown of the truly cold-hardy fountain grasses. Typically 2–3 ft. (60–90 cm) tall, with cultivated selections ranging from less than 1 ft. (30 cm) to more than 5 ft. (1.5 m). Leaves are narrow, to $^1/_2$ in. (12 mm) wide, green in summer turning golden yellow in autumn. Inflorescences are spikelike racemes, usually dense and cylindrical, resembling large foxtails. They are superb as cut materials for fresh bouquets. Flower color is dark purple (most common) to cream-white, and flowering begins as early as June or as late as September. Inflorescences remain attractive only into late fall or early winter, then begin to shatter. Easily grown in full sun or light shade on most soils. Moderately drought tolerant, best with regular moisture. Especially effective when planted in groups or masses or in decorative containers. Usually self-sows manageably. Propagate the species by seed or by division in spring, the cultivars by division only. Zone 6, sometimes colder.

'Cassian'. With dusky light brown flowers beginning in August, to 3 ft. (1 m) tall. Foliage turns rich gold with red tints in autumn. Named

Pennisetum alopecuroides 'Little Bunny' in late August in Pennsylvania.

Pennisetum alopecuroides 'Moudry' covered in morning dew in late October in the author's former Delaware garden.

Pennisetum 'Burgundy Giant' with *Verbena bonariensis* in late August in Colorado.

for German horticulturist Cassian Schmidt. Zone 6.

'Caudatum' (*P. caudatum* hort.). White-flowering fountain grass. Flowers are nearly white, beginning in August, to 4 ft. (1.2 m). A beautiful, underused cultivar. Zone 6.

'Hameln'. Flowers cream-white, beginning in late July. To 3 ft. (1 m) tall, which is at least 1 ft. (30 cm) shorter than the average species height. Excellent for groundcover massing. Zone 6.

'Little Bunny'. A true miniature, only 18 in. (45 cm) tall. Flowers in August. Originated as a seedling of 'Hameln'. Zone 6.

'Little Honey'. Leaves longitudinally striped white. Originated as a sport of 'Little Bunny' and is slightly smaller, usually only 1 ft. (30 cm) tall in bloom. Zone 6.

'Moudry'. Leaves relatively wide, to $7/16$ in. (11 mm), dark green, and very glossy, forming a neat, lustrous basal mound to 2 ft. (60 cm) tall. Blooms September to November, flowers exceptionally dark purple, extending on stiff stalks in late September. In some years, the inflorescences do not fully emerge from the foliage. This cultivar originated from seed introduced by the U.S. National Arboretum, Washington, D.C., from Japan, where populations of wide-leaved, late-blooming, dark-flowered plants are commonly native. Self-sows prolifically, especially if conditions are moist, and can seed heavily into lawns adjacent to flower beds. If grown near turf, it is advisable to cut back before seed is produced. Zone 6.

'National Arboretum'. Like 'Moudry' a wider-leaved fall-blooming variety that is particularly fertile and can be extremely invasive if conditions are suitably moist in and beyond the garden.

'Weserbergland'. Very similar to 'Hameln' but slightly larger, wider. Zone 6.

'Woodside'. Early blooming, flowers well in England. To 2 ft. (60 cm). A selection from Woodside, the garden of Mervyn Feesey of Barnstaple, England. Zone 6.

Pennisetum 'Burgundy Giant'
Giant burgundy fountain grass

The boldest-textured fountain grass, with bronze-burgundy leaves to $1\frac{3}{8}$ in. (35 mm) wide. Up-right, clump-forming, to 6 ft. (2 m). Blooms July to September, inflorescences colored like the foliage. Selected from plants growing at Marie Selby Botanical Gardens of unknown garden origin. Probably a variant of *P. macrostachyum*, a large species native to New Guinea, Borneo, and adjacent islands. 'Burgundy Giant' is very tender, requiring temperatures above 40°F (4°C). Makes a superb summer annual, planted in the ground or grown in a pot. Rapid-growing, reaching full height in a single summer even in zone 6. Prefers full sun, regular moisture. Usually does not set viable seed, but can easily be propagated from stem cuttings rooted in sand under mist. Zone 10.

Pennisetum incomptum
Spreading fountain grass

Native to northern China and the Himalayas. Spreads aggressively by rhizomes to form large masses to 4 ft. (1.2 m) tall. Leaves green to gray-green. Blooms late June, often continuing through August into September. Flowers greenish, drying light tan, on nearly upright stems. Racemes longer and much more slender than those of *P. alopecuroides*. Needs full sun but adapted to a wide range of soil and moisture conditions. Spreads too aggressively to be manageable in a mixed flower border, but is relatively early flowering, has good fall and winter presence, and can be an appropriate choice for a mass planting in difficult sites, such as traffic islands or in contained areas around buildings. Rhizomes persistent, can be difficult to eradicate once established. Zone 4.

Pennisetum macrourum
Fountain grass

Native to South Africa. Similar in most respects to *P. incomptum* but with racemes up to 2 in. (5 cm) longer. Zone 6.

Pennisetum orientale
Fountain grass

Native from central and southwestern Asia to northwestern India. One of the most striking hardy fountain grasses. Low growing, compact, and exceptionally floriferous when well grown. Blooms

Pennisetum incomptum is smartly held in check within a concrete-edged planting space surrounded by water in late August in Colorado.

Pennisetum orientale in light shade in early August in Maryland.

Pennisetum orientale 'Karly Rose' in early October in North Carolina.

Pennisetum orientale 'Tall Tales' in early August in trials in Pennsylvania.

over an unusually long period from late June into October. Inflorescences fluffy, nearly white with strong pearlescent pink tints in cool seasons. Requires well-drained soil, full sun, and warmth for best growth and flowering, but can be grown in part shade in warm regions. Insufficient summer sun reduces winter hardiness. Leaves green to gray-green. Densely clump-forming. When transplanting, take care that the crown of the plant is not at all below grade. Showy enough for specimen use, also superb in groups or masses or in a container. Rarely self-sows. Does not propagate easily by division, best from seed. Zone 6.

'**Karly Rose**'. Flowers strongly pink-tinted, 3–4 ft. (1–1.2 m). Zone 6.

'**Tall Tales**'. Unusually tall, to 6 ft. (1.8 m) in bloom. Flowers lightly pink tinted, quickly fading to white. Zone 6.

Pennisetum setaceum
Tender fountain grass

Native to tropical Africa, southwestern Asia, and Saudi Arabia. An old-fashioned garden

Pennisetum setaceum in late August in Pennsylvania.

Pennisetum setaceum 'Eaton Canyon' in mid-August in Pennsylvania.

Pennisetum setaceum 'Rubrum' in late September in Nebraska.

Pennisetum villosum in early August in northern Delaware.

favorite. Perennial in subtropical and tropical regions but usually treated as an annual grown from seed in colder zones. Clump-forming, erect to arching, to 5 ft. (1.5 m) tall, with purplish pink racemes nearly 15 in. (38 cm) long. Blooms July to September, superb for cut flowers. Leaves typically green. Taller and narrower than *P. alopecuroides*, this species sometimes requires staking in late summer, especially on moist, rich soils. Requires full sun. Self-sows in warm climates, and has escaped and naturalized in various parts of the world. In cold zones, propagate by seed sown indoors in late winter. New plants should not be set out until after danger of frost is past. Zone 9.

'Eaton Canyon' ('Cupreum Compactum', 'Rubrum Dwarf'). Compact purple fountain grass. Originated as a seedling of 'Rubrum'. Like 'Rubrum' in miniature, with a maximum height of 30 in. (75 cm) in flower.

'Rubrum' ('Atropurpureum', 'Cupreum', 'Purpureum'). Purple fountain grass. All parts of the plant a rich red-burgundy color. Leaves to ¾ in. (2 cm) wide. Upright, to 5 ft. (1.5 m) tall. Blooms late summer to first frost, with racemes more than 1 ft. (30 cm) long. Tender; does not survive prolonged temperatures below 40°F (4°C). Treated as a summer annual from plants held over in a greenhouse or purchased annually, the dramatically colorful grass is stunning as a specimen or in groups or masses. Rarely sets seed. Propagate by division. Zone 9.

Pennisetum villosum
Feathertop

Native to mountains in northeastern tropical Africa. Flowers nearly pure white, the racemes shorter, fuller, and more rounded than most fountain grasses. Prized by florists as a cut flower and equally attractive in the garden. Stems often lax. Tender, but more cold hardy than *P. setaceum*, occasionally surviving winters in zone 7. Best in full sun with regular moisture. Dramatic in mass or in a container. Propagate by seed. Zone 8.

PHALARIS
Canary grass (Grass family)

Comprised of about 15 annual or perennial species, native to cool north-temperate zones, including North America and Eurasia. Also native to Mediterranean regions and South America. *Phalaris canariensis*, canary grass, is widely cultivated for birdseed. A native of Mediterranean Europe, this annual has escaped and naturalized in various warm regions. Canary grass has short, wide flower panicles that are readily distinguished from the long, narrow panicles of reed canary grass, *P. arundinacea*, a perennial and the only species cultivated ornamentally, most often in its variegated-leaved forms.

Phalaris arundinacea
Reed canary grass

A cool-season, perennial species native to North America and Eurasia, usually in moist places. Plants of European origin were widely planted for forage and erosion control in North America, where they have since naturalized and become a major threat to marshes and other native wetlands. Unfortunately, there is no reliable method for distinguishing plants of European origin from plants of American origin. Control is difficult because it may result in inadvertent destruction of native plants. No herbicides are available. Frequent burning is one method of control in high-quality native wetlands, as is restoring water in wetlands to higher levels.

The typical plant has green leaves and is attractive but not showy. Stems are mostly upright, to 5 ft. (1.5 m) tall, flowering in June.

The variegated cultivars, which are all derived from plants of European origin, are quite distinct and are among the most dramatically variegated ornamental grasses. They often go partly or fully dormant in midsummer in hot climates. If cut back midseason, they produce a strong new flush of leaves that remains crisply attractive into early

Phalaris arundinacea in mid-July, naturalized along a flood plain in southeastern Pennsylvania.

winter. Flowers often detract from the overall appeal and are best cut back. Not particular about soils, but best with regular moisture, in full sun in cool climates or in part shade in hot regions. Self-sowing is very minor in the garden; however, all spread aggressively by rhizomes and require regular maintenance to keep contained. When properly sited, they are striking additions to the garden, useful as accents or groundcovers, and worth the effort required to control their spread. Also superb when grown in pots. Propagate cultivars by division in spring or fall. Zone 4.

'Feesey' ('Strawberries and Cream'). Named for British horticulturist and ornamental grass specialist Mervyn Feesey. Leaves green with prominent longitudinal stripes. Compared to 'Picta', the variegation is much stronger and clearer white, especially during cool periods of spring and autumn, when the foliage and stems are frequently and conspicuously tinted pink. More of a cool-season grower than 'Picta' and often suffers worse in extreme heat. Zone 4.

'Luteopicta' ('Aureovariegata'). Leaves with attractive cream-yellow stripes, especially in spring, darkening mostly to green in the heat of summer, especially in full sun. Zone 4.

'Picta' ('Elegantissima', f. *picta*, var. *picta*, var. *variegata*). Gardener's-garters, ribbon grass. A

Cool days bring suffusions of pink to the variegated foliage of *Phalaris arundinacea* 'Feesey' in Pennsylvania.

Phalaris arundinacea 'Luteopicta' in mid-April in Pennsylvania.

Phalaris arundinacea 'Picta' in late May in Connecticut.

Belying its problematic invasiveness, the silvery elegance of *Phragmites australis* makes a dramatic counterpoint to the rich reds of the deciduous forest in mid-October in New York.

Phragmites australis 'Variegatus' in late August in northern Germany.

popular favorite since the Victorian era, often persisting in gardens through successions of owners. Leaves green with dramatic cream-white stripes, never pink-flushed. Zone 4.

'Tricolor'. Nearly identical to 'Feesey' in having pink-flushed foliage in cool periods. The pink tones often persist into warmer weather, but the variegation is not quite as clear-white as that of 'Feesey'. Zone 4.

'Woods Dwarf' ('Dwarf's Garters'). Similar to 'Picta' but more compact, shorter. Zone 4.

PHRAGMITES
Reed (Grass family)

The genus name refers to the fencelike, screening effect created by dense stands of this large grass. Comprised of up to four very similar species of cosmopolitan distribution. Warm-season growers, all are strongly rhizomatous perennials of wet or moist habitats.

Phragmites australis
Common reed, carrizo

A huge, variable grass found on every continent except Antarctica and especially common in freshwater and brackish wetlands in temperate zones. Sturdy and upright, it usually grows 10–13 ft. (3–4 m) tall. Leaves are gray-green, to 2 in. (5 cm) wide. The large terminal inflorescences appear in August or September, opening golden tan to bronze-purple, drying to translucent silver. At its best, it provides a stunning, luminous balance to the brilliant autumn foliage of deciduous trees and shrubs and colorful fall flowers.

In places where it is indigenous, including North America, this species can be a stable component of native wetlands if the habitat is relatively undisturbed; however, during the twentieth century the species spread aggressively in countless temperate wetlands due to human activities including dredging, channeling, salting of roads, and waste discharge. The North American invasions are also due to the introduction of *P. australis* plants from other continents, with different genetic makeup disposing them to aggressive behavior in their transplanted locations. The herbicide Rodeo, containing glyphosate, is licensed for use over water and can be an effective temporary control on a local basis, but it is not a practical solution to the larger ecological dilemma. In any case, the typical species forms are too large and aggressive for most gardens. The variegated type is manageable and innocuous when grown as a container specimen. Zone 3.

'Variegatus'. Has dramatically yellow-striped leaves. To 8 ft. (2.4 m) tall if grown in full sun in wet soil, but much smaller if conditions are drier or if root growth is restricted. Effective at the edges of water garden pools or small ponds or grown in a container. Propagate by division in spring. Zone 4.

PLEURAPHIS
Galleta (Grass family)

Comprised of three species of perennial grasses native to dry regions in the western United States and northern Mexico. Formerly included in the genus *Hillaria*.

Pleuraphis jamesii
James' galleta

Native in deserts, canyons, and dry plains from California to Texas and Wyoming. Spreads by rhizomes to create a dense mass of upright stems 1–2 ft. (30–60 cm) tall. Leaves gray-green. A warm-season grower. Blooms late spring to early summer, the inflorescences narrow and upright. Very drought tolerant. Zone 8.

POA
Blue grass, meadowgrass (Grass family)

Comprised of approximately 500 annual and perennial grasses native mostly to cool temperate regions throughout the world. Includes the familiar wide-leaved lawn species, *P. pratensis*, Kentucky blue grass. Several other species have very fine textured leaves, some quite glaucous-blue and similar in appearance to their close relatives in the genus *Festuca*. Most are cool-season growers, best in full sun on well-drained soils. Propagate by seed or by division in spring.

Poa colensoi in mid-July in Scotland.

Pleuraphis jamesii in early evening light in mid-June in California.

Poa colensoi
New Zealand blue grass

Native to New Zealand. Densely tufted, clumping. Foliage very fine textured and glaucous-blue, to 1 ft. (30 cm) tall. Easily mistaken for blue fescue. Blooms late spring to early summer. Zone 7.

RHYNCHELYTRUM
Grass family

Includes 14 annual and perennial species native to savannas and other open habitats in tropical Africa, Madagascar, and Southeast Asia. Only the following is commonly grown ornamentally. It is a widespread, though usually innocuous, weed in the tropics.

Rhynchelytrum repens
Natal ruby grass

Native to open habitats in tropical Africa. Clumping, the narrow blue-green leaves forming a fine-textured mound. A tender and often short-lived perennial grown for its showy, pink to purple-red flowers, usually produced in summer or early autumn, to 2 ft. (80 cm) tall. Blooms through winter in mild climates or when grown under glass if provided sufficient moisture. The inflorescences are deeply colored when first opening, fading to light sandy pink. Easily grown on almost any soil. Best in full sun or very light shade. An innocuous weed of disturbed places in the tropics, this species is also naturalized on open sandy places in the southern United States,. Easily grown as an annual in cold zones and especially attractive as a potted specimen. Easily propagated by seed but may also be divided. Self-sows manageably in gardens in warm regions. Zone 8.

RHYNCHOSPORA
Beak-rush, white-top sedge (Sedge family)

The genus name refers to the elongated, beaklike seeds. Includes approximately 200 mainly perennial species native mostly to wet or moist habitats

Rhynchelytrum repens in mid-December in California.

in warm regions throughout the world. All are distinct in having conspicuously long, leafy bracts radiating from their inflorescences in a starlike pattern. The bracts are nearly white except at their tips and are quite ornamental, remaining attractive for months. Useful for fresh cut flowers or for drying. Perennial, spreading by rhizomes, these sedges make unusual, attractive additions to aquatic gardens and can also be grown in tubs or pots. They must not be allowed to dry out, or the bracts will scorch and turn brown. Propagate by seed or division.

Rhynchospora colorata
White-top sedge, star sedge

Native to moist sand, swamps, and pond edges in the eastern United States, mainly coastal, from Virginia to Florida and Texas and into Mexico. To 20 in. (50 cm) tall, blooming in summer, sometimes into winter in the warmer regions, with three to seven bracts of unequal lengths, white at their bases. Easily grown in full sun or light shade on moist soils or in shallow water to 2 in. (5 cm) deep. Tolerates brackish conditions. Runs by rhizomes to produce dense clusters. Zone 8.

Rhynchospora latifolia
White-top sedge, star sedge

Native to moist sand, savannas, pine woods, swamps, and pond edges in the southeastern United States, from the Carolinas south to Florida and Texas. Slightly taller and showier than *R. colorata*. To 32 in. (80 cm) tall, blooming in summer, sometimes into winter in the warmer regions, with six to ten bracts of unequal lengths, white at their bases. Easily grown in full sun or light shade on moist soils or in shallow water to 2 in. (5 cm) deep. Runs by rhizomes to produce dense clusters. Zone 8.

Rhynchospora nervosa
White-top sedge, star sedge

A tropical native of Central and South America and the Caribbean region. Similar to *R. colorata* and *R. latifolia* but larger, taller, to 5 ft. (1.5 m), and more tender. Zone 10.

Rhynchospora latifolia in early May in Alabama.

SACCHARUM
Plume grass, sugarcane (Grass family)

Comprised of approximately 40 perennial species native throughout the tropics and subtropics, extending into warm temperate regions. Most are found in moist habitats, though some grow on open hillsides. Sugarcane, *S. officinarum*, is widely cultivated in warm regions for the production of sugar, and selections with colored stems are also occasionally grown for ornament. Ravenna grass, *S. ravennae*, is widely grown in temperate gardens. Several North American natives are still largely unknown in gardens but have genuine ornamental potential. The North American species are similar in their narrow, upright form and can be used to make a strong vertical impact even in relatively small spaces. They are mostly clump-forming. All have large, plumy inflorescences that remain translucent and attractive throughout winter, and many have rich autumn foliage color. All are warm-season growers. Propagate by division in spring or by seed.

Saccharum alopecuroidum
Silver plume grass

Native to open, moist, sandy woods in eastern United States. Distinct from many other North American natives in its strong preference for shaded habitats. The inflorescences also differ, being strongly silver even when first opening in August or September, to 1 ft. (30 cm) long. To 10 ft. (3 m) tall, leaves green, to 1 in. (25 mm) wide, with little significant autumn color. An interesting choice of vertical accent for woodland gardens. Self-sows manageably. Zone 7.

Saccharum arundinaceum
Hardy sugarcane

Native to India and Southeast Asia, where it is sometimes used in paper manufacture. Relatively little known to gardeners, but with strong ornamental potential. Material collected in China has proved hardy into zone 6. Leaves broad, gray-green. Blooms in late summer or early autumn, the large open panicles light pink at first, fading

Saccharum arundinaceum in early October in North Carolina.

Saccharum contortum (left) and *S. alopecuroidum* (right) in the author's Pennsylvania garden in late October.

Saccharum contortum in early September (above) and in mid October (below) in the author's Pennsylvania garden.

to silver, to 7 ft. (2.1 m) tall or more. Best in full sun. Zone 6.

Saccharum contortum
Bent-awn plume grass

Native to open ground on the coastal plain or in moist sandy pinelands from Delaware south to Florida and Texas, north to Tennessee and Oklahoma. Clump-forming and narrowly upright to 10 ft. (3 m) tall. Leaves to ¾ in. (2 cm) wide, green in summer turning various shades of purple, bronze, and orange-red in autumn. The foliage has a distinct reddish coloration even in winter. The narrow, strictly upright plumes appear in September, standing about 2 ft. (60 cm) above the uppermost leaves. Reddish brown at first, the flower clusters become lighter upon drying. The awns have a characteristic twist. Best in full sun or light shade on moist soils. Grow in clay or even periodically wet soil. Self-sows to a minor extent in northern regions, heavily in southern regions. Zone 6.

Saccharum giganteum in a moist Virginia woodland in mid-September.

Saccharum officinarum 'Pele's Smoke' in early February in California.

Saccharum giganteum
Giant plume grass, sugarcane plume grass

Native on moist soil, mainly on the coastal plain from New York south to Florida and Texas, north to Kentucky. The largest of the North American native species but still considerably smaller than ravenna grass, *S. ravennae*. Stems mostly upright, to 10 ft. (3 m) tall or more, spreading modestly by rhizomes. Blooms in late summer or early autumn, the inflorescences strongly pink-red at first, drying to light pink, eventually translucent and silvery in winter. Plumes large and fluffy, the fullest of the North American natives. Autumn foliage colors include dark red and bronze-purple. Zone 6.

Saccharum officinarum
Sugarcane

Native origin unknown, possibly Southeast Asia. Grown for centuries and still the primary source of

Saccharum ravennae in mid-October in Pennsylvania.

the world's sugar, this large, tender tropical grass is increasingly finding its way into ornamental gardens as selections with colored leaves and stems become more available. Capable of reaching 20 ft. (6 m) tall in tropical climates, it rarely grows more than 8 ft. (2.4 m) when planted as a summer annual in cooler zones. Usually does not bloom under these conditions. This warm-season grower thrives in full sun and warm, moist conditions, and is easily grown in a large container, providing an interesting tropical accent. Culms are to 2 in. (5 cm) in diameter. Many colored selections are without reliable names. Propagate by division or by rooting stem sections. Zone 10.

'Pele's Smoke'. Purple-stemmed sugarcane. Similar or identical to 'Violaceum'.

'Violaceum'. Purple-stemmed sugarcane. Foliage smoky purple. Stems shiny mahogany-purple with distinct cream-colored bands marking the nodes, remaining attractive into winter in colder zones, after the foliage has died back due to frosts.

Saccharum ravennae
Ravenna grass
Native to northern Africa and the Mediterranean region. Sometimes called hardy pampas grass in areas too cold to sustain the true pampas grass, *Cortaderia selloana*. Among the largest and most striking of the cold-hardy ornamental grasses.

Upright and clumping, with leaves to 1 in. (25 mm) wide, gray-green, forming a large basal mound to 4 ft. (1.2 m) tall. Blooms only in regions with long, warm growing seasons. Large, plumy inflorescences are produced in late August or early September, on stout, upright-divergent stems to 14 ft. (4.2 m) tall. The flowers are slightly pink-tinted when first opening, quickly turning lustrous silver, standing tall and remaining attractive through winter. Superb for fresh or dried flower arrangements, best cut before fully expanded. The flowering stems become conspicuously red-tinted in late summer, and in autumn the foliage assumes pleasing orange tones.

Requires full sun but is otherwise undemanding as to site and soil conditions. Very drought tolerant once established. Excess moisture or fertility encourages lax growth and causes flowering stems to fall outward to the ground unless staked or tied. Grows for many years with little maintenance other than annual cutting back, but clumps eventually die out in the center and should be renewed by division in spring. May also be started from seed. Self-sows in very warm regions.

A magnificent specimen for sheer size and the vertical, shining effect of its ample plumes. Also effective in groupings in larger gardens. Zone 6.

SCHIZACHYRIUM
Grass family
Comprised of a single North American species related to *Andropogon*. In *Schizachyrium* each raceme is located at the end of a slender peduncle, which extends noticeably from each branching point of the stem, whereas the racemes of *Andropogon* are clustered, two to four on each peduncle, and the peduncles are short and mostly enclosed by the leaf sheaths.

Schizachyrium scoparium
Little bluestem, prairie beard grass
Native to prairies and open woods, dry fields, and hills in North America. Originally a characteristic grass of the American tallgrass prairie, wide-ranging, tolerant of average moisture to extremely dry conditions, and both acid and alkaline soils. Unlike its close relative, *Andropogon virginicus*, little bluestem is a valuable forage grass and has been widely planted for this reason since the demise of the great prairies.

Strictly clump-forming, it is fine-textured but not particularly little, growing from 2–4 ft. (60–120 cm) tall. It is little only in comparison to big bluestem, *Andropogon gerardii*, which can reach 8 ft. (2.4 m). Form varies from rigidly erect to lax and arching. Summer foliage color varies from bright green to strongly glaucous and light blue, often with conspicuous purple tints. Fall

Schizachyrium scoparium in early October in a Pennsylvania meadow with native asters (*Aster novae-angliae*) and goldenrods (*Solidago* species) blooming in the background.

The inflorescences of *Schizachyrium scoparium* (right) are individually held out from the stems on slender branches, unlike the densely clustered inflorescences of *Andropogon virginicus* (left).

By mid-August, pink and magenta highlights are suffused through the gray-blue foliage of *Schizachyrium scoparium* 'The Blues' in Pennsylvania.

In late October, a deeper red plant of *Schizachyrium scoparium* is easily distinguished among a hillside population in Pennsylvania.

Schizachyrium scoparium 'The Blues' in early August in Pennsylvania.

and winter color varies from tan to copper-orange to dark orange-red. Plants with strongly glaucous-blue summer foliage have the most pronounced deep red coloring in autumn and winter. Blooms in late summer, the inflorescences delicate and inconspicuous until they dry, becoming silvery and noticeably attractive when side-lit or back-lit by the autumn or winter sun. Remains attractive through winter, even after snows.

Requires full sun, prefers good drainage or sloping ground. Does not persist on highly fertile soils or in excessively moist conditions, and suffers if the crowns are crowded by mulch. Ideal for managed meadows, where it coexists happily with prairie wildflowers as long as it is not shaded. The blue-leaved selections are showy enough to merit consideration even in highly designed landscapes. Propagate by seed or by division in spring. Zone 3.

'Aldous'. A seed cultivar originally developed for forage, producing a high percentage of tall, blue-leaved plants.

'Stars & Stripes'. Leaves striped cream-yellow.

'The Blues'. A clonal cultivar with strongly glaucous, light blue stems. Selected from seedlings of 'Aldous'. Propagate by division only. Zone 3.

SCHOENOPLECTUS
Bulrush, clubrush (Sedge family)

Comprised of approximately 80 annual and perennial species of cosmopolitan distribution in aquatic and semi-aquatic habitats. Many species have been included in the closely related genus *Scirpus*. The great bulrush, *Schoenoplectus tabernaemontani*, has long been cultivated ornamentally in water gardens; however, many other species deserve further attention. All are warm-season growers.

Schoenoplectus subterminalis
Swaying-rush

Aquatic, native to ponds and slow-moving, often acid waters, and to bogs and peaty shores across northern North America. A subtly beautiful plant, growing mostly submersed in up to 5 ft. (1.5 m) of water, the long, threadlike, lime-green leaves and stems float just beneath the water's surface, gently revealing undulations in the current. The specific epithet *subterminalis* refers to the tiny inflorescences, which are just below the tips of stems that extend a few inches out of water at flowering time in midsummer. Runs by rhizomes. Not suited to smaller aquatic gardens, but truly worth establishing, enhancing, or conserving in larger landscapes. Propagate by seed or division. Zone 4.

Schoenoplectus tabernaemontani
Great bulrush, clubrush

Of cosmopolitan distribution in freshwater and brackish rivers, lakes, and ponds. Mostly clump-forming, with rushlike, upright stems carrying on the usual photosynthetic functions of leaves and bearing clusters of brownish flowers, usually in their upper portion. Though the variegated cultivars are most often grown, the simple grace of the typical, dark green stems can be attractive at the edge of ponds or pools in water gardens, especially as textural foils for broad-leaved waterlilies and other aquatics. Best on neutral to acid soils in shallow water, with full sun exposure. Propagate by division in spring.

'**Albescens**'. White bulrush. Stems nearly white, with only narrow longitudinal stripes of green, to 5 ft. (1.5 m). Zone 5.

'**Golden Spears**'. Stems fully yellow in spring, fading to green as the season progresses. Zone 5.

'**Zebrinus**'. Zebra bulrush. Stems dark green with vivid light yellow horizontal bands. Zone 5.

Mostly submersed, *Schoenoplectus subterminalis* sways gently with the Wading River's slow-moving currents in early July in the New Jersey pine barrens.

Schoenoplectus tabernaemontani 'Albescens' in mid-July in Scotland.

Schoenoplectus tabernaemontani 'Zebrinus' in early June in Pennsylvania.

Schoenoplectus tabernaemontani in native habitat in northern Delaware.

Scirpus cyperinus in late August with tickseed sunflower, *Bidens polylepis*, in northern Delaware.

SCIRPUS
Sedge family

Includes approximately 100 perennial species of cosmopolitan distribution in moist habitats. Warm-season growers, they usually have well-developed leaves and flowers in terminal panicles, which are sometimes showy. Closely related to the genera *Isolepis* and *Schoenoplectus* (which see).

Scirpus cyperinus
Wool grass

Native to wet meadows and swamps in northeastern North America. Very ornamental, with large woolly inflorescences on erect stems to 5 ft. (1.5 m) tall. Blooms in midsummer, the flowers green at first, becoming softly woolly and light brown as seeds mature in late summer. Remains upright and attractive throughout winter. Forms dense tussocks, with many arching basal leaves in summer. Easily grown on moist or periodically wet soils in full sun or light shade. Self-

sows and thus ideal for naturalizing. Propagate by seed or by division in spring. Zone 4.

SESLERIA
Moor grass (Grass family)

Named for Leonardo Sesler, an eighteenth-century Venetian physician who owned a botanic garden. Includes approximately 25 species native to Europe, often in mountainous areas, centered in the Balkans. Most are densely tufted perennials with evergreen or semi-evergreen foliage. They are frequently overlooked because they lack showy flowers; however, many are tough, long-lived plants of easy culture that are superbly suited for groundcover use, in full sun to as much as half shade. Most are very drought tolerant once established. They offer a variety of sizes and foliage colors in shades of yellow-green to blue-green. Most are very cold hardy and tolerant of alkaline soils. Propagate by seed or by division in spring or fall.

Sesleria autumnalis in mid-August in the author's Pennsylvania garden.

Sesleria caerulea in early May in Pennsylvania.

Sesleria autumnalis
Autumn moor grass

Native from northeastern Italy to Albania. Distinguished from most other species by its late summer to fall flowering period and by its nearly lime-green foliage. Leaves to ³⁄₈ in. (9 mm) wide. The inflorescences are conspicuous and attractive, held erect above the foliage to 20 in. (50 cm), opening silvery-white. Zone 4.

Sesleria caerulea
Blue moor grass

Native to Europe, including the British Isles, often in calcareous grasslands, limestone rock-crevices, and screes. Low-growing, forming basal mounds of strongly blue-green foliage to 8 in. (20 cm) tall. To ³⁄₁₆ in. (4 mm) wide, the leaves are two-toned: strongly glaucous-blue on their upper surfaces with dark green undersides. Due to the way the foliage lays, both colors are always visible. Blooms April to May, the small spikelike panicles held above the foliage on slender stalks. Flowers are blackish at first, with light yellow pollen sacs, turning mostly green and becoming inconspicuous.

Sesleria heufleriana in early May in Pennsylvania.

The foliage is nearly evergreen even to zone 6. Zone 4.

Sesleria heufleriana
Blue-green moor grass

Native to southeastern Europe. Very similar to blue moor grass but larger, taller, and less blue. The upper surfaces of the leaves are mostly green in early spring, becoming noticeably glaucous-blue by early summer and remaining so through autumn and winter. The early spring flowers are black with cream-yellow pollen sacs, held above the foliage on slender stalks that continue to grow taller as the seed matures and then fall to the sides, becoming inconspicuous. The foliage forms neat tufted mounds to 15 in. (38 cm) tall and is semi-evergreen even in colder climates. Zone 4.

Sesleria nitida
Gray moor grass

Native to central and southern Italy and Sicily. Appears strongly gray-blue in the landscape. The leaves are two-toned, like those of *S. caerulea*

Sesleria nitida in mid-May in Maryland.

and *S. heufleriana*, but they lay flat, with the strongly glaucous upper surfaces always visible. *Sesleria nitida* is the tallest of the three species, forming a flowing mound of foliage to 20 in. (50 cm) tall, overtopped in early spring by nearly black flower panicles similar to the other spring-flowering species. Leaves to ¼ in. (6 mm) wide, the foliage semi-evergreen. Zone 4.

SETARIA
Foxtail (Grass family)

The genus name refers to the bristlelike inflorescence. Includes approximately 100 annual and perennial species of open grasslands and woodlands, widely distributed in tropical, subtropical, and temperate zones. Many of the annual foxtails are cosmopolitan weeds and, although sometimes attractive, are only occasionally grown ornamentally. The following perennial species is a tender tropical, grown mostly for its bold, palm-like foliage.

Setaria palmifolia in late summer.

Setaria palmifolia
Palm grass

Native to tropical Asia. A coarse-textured perennial, growing to 10 ft. (3 m) tall in tropical climates. The rich green leaves are 3–5 in. (7.5–12 cm) wide and conspicuously pleated. The inflorescences are only subtly interesting. Cylindrical and green, they extend above or arch outward from the foliage on slender green stems. Palm grass is often displayed as a conservatory specimen, but also makes an interesting tropical accent if grown in a container placed in the garden during warm periods. It may also be planted in the ground for summer and removed to protection in winter. Does not tolerate prolonged temperatures below 40°F (4°C). Grows to 5 ft. (1.5 m) tall in a single summer if provided plenty of sun and moisture. Propagate by division. Zone 9.

SORGHASTRUM
Indian grass, wood grass (Grass family)

The genus name means "imitation sorghum," referring to the resemblance to sorghum. Includes approximately 15 annual and perennial species native to the Americas and tropical Africa. A characteristic North American tallgrass prairie species, *S. nutans*, is very important ornamentally. Two less-known southeastern United States species deserve further evaluation in gardens.

Sorghastrum nutans
Indian grass

The second most-prevalent species in the once-vast North American tallgrass prairie. A warm-season grower, blooming in late summer. Widely distributed in prairies, dry slopes, and open woods from Quebec to Mexico. Plants of central prairie provenance tend to have broad leaves, to ½ in. (12 mm) wide, which are frequently glaucous and bluish. They also tend to be tall, to 7 ft. (2.1 m) or more when in flower. As the species reaches the eastern part of its range the foliage tends to be narrower and completely green, and ultimate height is usually closer to 5 ft. (1.5 m). Narrow green-leaved

Bright yellow anthers and light yellow feathery stigmas extend from the coppery awned spikelets of *Sorghastrum nutans* in mid-August in eastern Pennsylvania.

Sorghastrum nutans is bright golden orange in mid-October in eastern Pennsylvania.

plants tend to be more upright than wide-leaved glaucous types, especially if conditions are at all shaded. Autumn foliage color is yellow on glaucous-leaved plants and bright orange on green-leaved individuals. The showy flower panicles usually appear in August and are copper-colored with conspicuous bright yellow pollen sacs. Loose and open at first, the inflorescences narrow upon drying, becoming light chestnut brown and translucent and remaining attractive through most of winter. They make good cut flowers, fresh or dried.

Easy to grow on a wide range of soils, including heavy clay. Best in full sun. Grows taller with moisture but is drought tolerant once established. Self-sows prolifically. Requires little maintenance other than cutting back annually, which is best done in late winter or early spring. Propagate by seed or division.

'Osage'. A seed cultivar developed primarily for forage and pasture use, prairie origin. Leaves relatively wide and often glaucous-blue. Plants are frequently lax-stemmed when mature. Zone 4.

Gray-blue-leafed *Sorghastrum nutans* 'Sioux Blue' (left) and a typical green-leafed plant of *S. nutans* (right) in late August in Pennsylvania.

'Sioux Blue'. Blue Indian grass. A clonal cultivar selected from a seedling of 'Osage' after extensive evaluation in Longwood Gardens' research nursery. Chosen for its powder-blue foliage and erect form. When grown in full sun, it remains upright throughout the growing season and through most of winter. Leaves to $^1/_2$ in. (12 mm) wide, flowering stems to 6 ft. (2 m). Foliage turns yellow in late fall. Heat tolerant and free of the foliar rust diseases that sometimes afflict the glaucous-leaved cultivars of *Panicum virgatum*, and a better choice for gardens in the warm southeastern United States. Zone 4.

Sorghastrum secundatum
Drooping wood grass

Native to pine and oak-pine barrens, on mostly sandy soils, from South Carolina to Florida and Texas. Similar to *S. nutans* but shorter and with strongly one-sided panicles on arching stems usually less than 5 ft. (1.5 m) tall. Blooms in late summer. Zone 7, possibly colder.

SPARTINA
Cordgrass (Grass family)

Includes approximately 15 perennial species native almost exclusively to wet or moist habitats on both coasts of North and South America and to the Atlantic coasts of Africa and Europe, especially in temperate and subtropical zones. Most spread by rhizomes to form extensive colonies, often to the exclusion of other plants. They are critically important soil builders and stabilizers in coastal and interior marshes. Most cordgrasses grow in brackish or saline environments.

Spartina bakeri
Sand cordgrass

Unlike many cordgrasses, this species is not a marsh dweller. It grows natively in full sun and sandy, often dry soil in South Carolina, Georgia, Florida, and Texas. Clump-forming and fine-textured, with medium-green leaves only $^1/_4$ in. (6 mm) wide, sand cordgrass forms a dense mound 3–6 ft. (90–180 cm) tall. Sturdy and long-lived,

Spartina bakeri in early February in Florida.

Spartina pectinata 'Aureomarginata' in late June in eastern Pennsylvania.

this grass may be used as a hedge or in other ways, singly or in massed plantings, to define garden spaces. It is increasingly grown as an ornamental in warmer regions. Propagates easily by seed. Zone 8, possibly colder.

Spartina pectinata
Prairie cordgrass

Native mostly to freshwater marshes and wet prairies throughout the northern United States, extending into brackish areas near the Atlantic coast. Spreads rapidly by rhizomes, with strong upright to arching stems. A warm-season grower, blooming in late July and August, producing stiff, open panicles. To 7 ft. (2.1 m) tall in flower. Leaves to ⅝ in. (15 mm) wide, pendent, dark green, and glossy. The usual green-leaved plant is not often cultivated for ornament, but is important in habitat restoration and conservation. Grows best in full sun on moist soils but tolerates average or dry soils, where its spreading is greatly reduced. Also salt tolerant. Propagate by seed or division. Zone 4.

Spodiopogon sibiricus in early August in Maryland.

The delicate inflorescences of Sporobolus airoides begin to open in mid-June California.

'Aureomarginata' ('Variegata'). Differs from the species only in having bright yellow variegated leaf margins. Propagate by division. Zone 4.

SPODIOPOGON
Grass family

The genus name means "ashen beard," referring to the gray hairs surrounding the flower spikes and imparting a grayish color to the inflorescences. Includes nine mostly perennial species native to temperate and subtropical Asia. Only the following is commonly cultivated ornamentally.

Spodiopogon sibiricus
Siberian graybeard, o-abura-suzuki

Native to slopes and mountains in Japan, Korea, Manchuria, and China, as well as Siberia, where it frequently grows in forest glades and among shrubs. Clump-forming and upright, to 4 ft. (1.2 m) tall in flower, with a neatly rounded form. Erect terminal panicles are produced in July and August. Though they lack appreciable color, they are covered with small hairs that glow when side-lit or back-lit by the sun. The inflorescences are

effective until late October. The thin, flat leaves are medium green, to ⅝ in. (15 mm) wide, held nearly horizontal, often turning rich red and burgundy in autumn, or, in years with hard frosts, turning directly from green to brown. Prefers light shade but grows well in full sun if provided adequate moisture. Not drought tolerant. Grows in fairly dense shade, but its form will be much looser, often attractively so. Easily grown in a shrub border. Effective as a specimen or in sweeps and masses. Propagate by seed or by division in spring. Zone 4.

'West Lake'. From material collected in China. Zone 4.

SPOROBOLUS
Dropseed (Grass family)

Comprised of approximately 100 annual and perennial species of cosmopolitan distribution in temperate, subtropical, and tropical regions, in a wide range of habitats but most frequently growing on open savannas. All are warm-season bunchgrasses. Only prairie dropseed, S. hetero-lepis, is commonly cultivated as an ornamental. A

A ten-year-old clump of
Sporobolus heterolepis
in Pennsylvania
in mid-July.

Sporobolus heterolepis in
the author's Pennsylvania
garden in late August.

The warm autumn tones of
Sporobolus heterolepis are
accentuated by early
November sunlight in the
author's Pennsylvania garden.

number of other species hold promise. Those listed below make fine garden plants.

Sporobolus airoides
Alkali sacaton, alkali dropseed

Native to valleys and meadows, especially on alkaline soils, from South Dakota and Missouri west to eastern Washington, south to southern California, Texas, and Mexico. Forms from the eastern part of this range tend to be larger, more coarsely textured, and showier in bloom. Clump-forming, with gray-green leaves to ¼ in. (6 mm) wide, forming a loose flowing mound to 1–3 ft. (30–90 cm) tall. The foliage turns yellow in autumn then light tan during winter. Usually blooms April to July, but occasionally as late as October, the open flower panicles upright or arching, to 5 ft. (1.5 m) tall, opening with a strong pink cast, drying to silver. Deep-rooted, durable, and drought tolerant. Easy to grow on a wide range of soils from sands to heavy clays. Tolerates alkaline conditions. Best propagated by seed. Zone 5, probably colder.

Sporobolus wrightii in mid-July in a trial in North Carolina.

Sporobolus heterolepis
Prairie dropseed

Native to North American prairies. Among the most elegant and refined prairie grasses, with threadlike leaves just over ¹⁄₁₆ in. (< 2 mm) wide, producing a dense, flowing mound of the finest texture, to 15 in. (38 cm) tall. Summer color is a glossy, medium green. In October or early November, the entire clump turns deep orange, then fades to a light copper color during winter. Appearing in August or September, delicate, open panicles are held high above the foliage on very slender stalks to 30 in. (75 cm) tall. The inflorescences are noticeably attractive when back-lit, and, most unusually, they are delicately scented. Strictly clump-forming, deep-rooted, and extraordinarily drought tolerant once established. Slow-growing, often requiring four years or more to attain mature size but worth the wait. This long-lived, trouble-free plant thrives for decades without any center dieback or need for renewal. For this reason, it is a superb choice for small-scale or large-scale groundcover use. Easy to grow on most soils, including heavy clay, in full sun or light shade. Plentiful moisture and a fertile soil hasten growth but are not necessary. Sufficiently refined to merit a place in the formal garden, but also a natural for prairie and meadow gardens. Best propagated by seed. Division is possible but difficult because this grass produces an extremely dense crown. Zone 4.

'Wisconsin'. Selected for reliable bloom in Europe from material of Wisconsin provenance supplied by Prairie Nursery. Zone 4.

Sporobolus wrightii
Big sacaton, giant sacaton

Native from southeastern Arizona east to western Texas and Oklahoma south to northern Mexico, growing most often in semidesert habitats but also in moister situations on floodplains and around desert lakes and marshes. One of the largest species in the genus, this clump-former grows to 3–6 ft. (90–180 cm) in flower. It deserves more attention by gardeners. Zone 7, likely colder.

STENOTAPHRUM
Grass family

The genus name means "narrow trench," referring to the depression in the axis of the flower raceme. Comprised of seven annual and perennial, mostly stoloniferous species native to New and Old World tropics. Only the following is significant to gardens.

Stenotaphrum secundatum
St. Augustine grass

Native from South Carolina to Florida and Texas and into tropical America. Typically green-leaved, this stoloniferous perennial species is widely cultivated as a coarse-textured lawn grass in warm zones, and has naturalized and escaped in some regions. Zone 9.

'Variegatum'. Leaves longitudinally striped cream-white. Often cultivated for use in hanging baskets or planters, treated as an annual in colder climates. Easily rooted from stem cuttings. Rarely used in larger landscapes, though it was used to stunning effect by Brazilian landscape architect Roberto Burle Marx, who created huge undulating sweeps of this variegated selection alternating with the green form. Zone 9.

STIPA
Needle grass, spear grass (Grass family)

This genus was once defined very broadly and included many diverse species. Taxonomic research now supports a narrower view of *Stipa* and has resulted in transfers of many species to other genera, including *Achnatherum*, *Austrostipa*, *Hesperostipa*, and *Nassella*. The species remaining in *Stipa* are mostly sun-loving perennials native to steppes and rocky slopes in temperate and warm temperate regions. Most have characteristically long awns, which add to the beauty and translucency of their inflorescences. All are tufted clump-formers with primarily basal foliage. They require good drainage, and most are cool-season growers, preferring full sun but low humidity. Propagate by seed.

Stipa barbata
Feather grass

Native to southern Europe. Slender and upright-arching, to 30 in. (75 cm) tall, with silvery awns

Stipa barbata in mid-July in England.

Stipa capillata in late August in Germany.

Stipa gigantea in late August in Germany.

nearly 7¹/₂ in. (19 cm) long, streaming from the tips of the flower stems. Blooms July to August. Zone 8.

Stipa capillata

Native to central and southern Europe and Asia. Slender and nearly erect, to 32 in. (80 cm) tall, with relatively straight, silvery awns to 5 in. (12 cm) long. Blooms July to August. Zone 6.

Stipa gigantea
Giant feather grass, giant-oat

Native to Spain, Portugal, and Morocco. The largest feather grass and one of the most elegant and stately ornamental grasses. Leaves narrow, ¹/₈ in. (3 mm) wide, forming large tufts of basal foliage to 20 in. (50 cm) tall, evergreen in mild climates. Blooms June to August, the loose, open panicles held high above the foliage on stems to 8 ft. (2.4 m) tall. The spikelets are golden, with awns to 5 in. (12 cm) long, and are especially dramatic when moving with a summer breeze lit by

the sun. Superb for cut or dried arrangements. This cool-season grower is at its best in England, northern Europe, and the Pacific Northwest, but can be grown satisfactorily in areas with hot, humid summers if provided a sunny site and very well drained soil. Does not survive waterlogged winter conditions. Zone 6.

Stipa pennata
European feather grass

Native from southern and central Europe into the Himalayas. Leaves narrow, gray-green, forming a neat basal mound. Flowering stems to 30 in. (75 cm) tall, with silvery awns to 8 in. (20 cm) long. Zone 6.

THEMEDA
Grass family

Includes as many as 19 annual and perennial species native to open savannas mostly in eastern Asia, but also in Old World tropics and subtropics. Only the following species is grown ornamentally.

Themeda japonica in mid-August in Maryland.

Themeda japonica in early November in Maryland.

Themeda japonica
Japanese themeda, megarukaya

Native to lowlands and low mountains in Japan, as well as Korea, Manchuria, China, and India. Often overlooked because it lacks obvious flowers; however, it possesses a unique sculptural form that can be an intriguing addition to the garden. Strictly clumping, with leafy stems radiating from the base to create a broad fountain of foliage to 5 ft. (1.5 m) tall. Leaves to ¼ in. (6 mm) wide, bright green in summer turning rich golden orange by early November. By midwinter, the leaves have become light copper-brown and the stems golden yellow. Blooms in late summer, the flowers clustered along the upper portions of the stems and relatively insignificant. This warm-season grass begins growth late in spring but does not mind strong sun, heat, or humidity. Easy to grow on a broad range of soils and extremely drought tolerant once established. Propagate by seed or by division in spring. Effective singly or in groups or masses, this reliably attractive, long-lived grass is still little known and underappreciated. Zone 4.

THYSANOLAENA
Grass family

The genus name means "tassel cloak," referring to the fringe on the fertile lemmas (the lower, outer bracts of the flower). Comprised of one large perennial species native to tropical Asia.

Thysanolaena maxima

Native to open habitats, often in the mountains, in tropical Asia. A huge grass, forming a dense clump with upright to arching stems to 10 ft. (3 m) tall and equally wide or wider. It is sometimes grown in tropical regions for screening. The evergreen leaves are deep, glossy green, to 2¾ in. (7 cm) wide, tapering to narrow points, clothing the stems up to the base of the large, terminal panicles. This species was a favorite of Brazilian landscape architect Roberto Burle Marx, who valued it for its bold texture and graceful plumes. A true tropical, it is winter hardy only in frost-free zones but makes a superb conservatory specimen in colder regions or can be grown in a large container for summer

Thysanolaena maxima in Brazil.

Tridens flavus in late August in eastern Pennsylvania.

Tripsacum dactyloides in late June in northern Delaware.

and removed to protection in winter. Requires regular moisture. Propagate by division or seed. Zone 10.

TRIDENS
Grass family

Includes 18 perennial species native to open woodlands and plains in eastern North America south to Argentina and Angola. Only the following species is grown ornamentally.

Tridens flavus
Purpletop, tall redtop

Native to meadows, fields, and openings and borders of woods in eastern North America. Best known for the purple top it puts on eastern U.S. meadows and old fields in late summer. Upright and clump-forming, usually 4 ft. (1.2 m) tall in flower. The foliage is relatively coarse-textured, with medium-green leaves to ⅝ in. (15

mm) wide. Blooms August to September, the open panicles initially metallic red-purple, drying to silvery-tan, standing tall above the foliage through winter and into the following spring. Attractive as a cut flower. The foliage becomes bronze-purple tinted in autumn. Prefers full sun or light shade. Grows on a wide range of soils and is tolerant of moist or dry conditions. Self-sows readily and thus is best suited to naturalizing in meadows or meadow gardens, in large sweeps and masses. Propagate by seed or division. Zone 4.

TRIPSACUM
Gama grass (Grass family)

Includes 13 species native mainly to open woodlands and damp edges from North America south to Paraguay, but most common in Central America. The following species are attractive and sometimes grown ornamentally.

Tripsacum dactyloides
Eastern gama grass, Fakahatchee grass

Native to wet swales, streambanks, and other moist places from Massachusetts west to Nebraska and south to Florida and Texas. A large, coarse, rhizomatous grass to 8 ft. (2.4 m) tall in flower. Leaves gray-green with a prominent white midrib, to 1⅛ in. (3 cm) wide, mostly basal. Blooms June to September, the inflorescence consisting of narrowly cylindrical structures with female spikelets in the lower portion and males in the upper. The feathery pink stigmas produced by the female spikelets are long and conspicuous. Easily grown in full sun or light shade and most soils. Prefers moisture but fairly drought tolerant. Use caution when handling: the leaf margins are quite sharp and can cause razorlike cuts. Propagate by seed or division. Zone 5.

Tripsacum floridanum
Florida gama grass, dwarf Fakahatchee grass

Native only to rocky pinelands in southern Florida, this species is similar to eastern gama grass, *T. dactyloides*, but smaller and more compact in all respects. It is much finer textured, with leaves approximately ⅛ in. (3 mm) wide. It forms a clump of mounded foliage 1–1½ ft. (30–50 cm) high, overtopped by the slender, relatively inconspicuous flower stalks. Prefers full sun. Very drought tolerant. Zone 9, possibly colder.

TYPHA
Cat-tail, reedmace, bulrush (Cat-tail family)

The only genus in the cat-tail family, comprised of 10 to 15 species native to marshes and similar wetland habitats throughout the world's temperate and tropical regions. They spread by stout rhizomes to form dense colonies, often excluding other species, but providing important cover for wildlife. All cat-tails can be easily managed by growing in tubs or containers.

The flat, swordlike leaves are thick, slightly spongy, and nearly vertical, arising from the base of the plant. Usually gray-green in summer, they frequently turn bright yellow or gold in autumn. Warm-season growers, cat-tails typically bloom in

Tripsacum floridanum in mid-February in Florida.

mid to late summer. The densely packed female spikes turn from green to rich brown in color as the seeds mature; the spikes are widely popular for cut flower arrangements. The fruiting spikes usually remain intact until December and are often a beautiful part of snowy, winter landscapes. Propagate by division of the rhizome or by seed.

Typha angustifolia
Narrow-leaved cat-tail, lesser bulrush
Native to the Americas, Europe, and Asia. Flowering stems to 6 ft. (2 m) tall. Male and female segments of the inflorescence are separated by a sterile, naked section. Mature female spikes brown, to ⅝ in. (15 mm) in diameter. Generally more slender and graceful than *T. latifolia*, though intermediate hybrids known as *T. glauca* exist. These hybrids are mostly seed-sterile but can form large colonies by vegetative spread. Zone 3.

Typha latifolia
Common cat-tail, broad-leafed cat-tail
Native to North America, Europe, and Asia. Flowering stems to 10 ft. (3 m) tall. Male and female

Typha latifolia in late June in northern Delaware.

Typha latifolia in late October in eastern Pennsylvania.

Typha latifolia 'Variegata' in mid-August in Pennsylvania.

Typha angustifolia in late March in Michigan.

Typha minima in mid-May in Pennsylvania.

segments of the inflorescence continuous, without a sterile section. Mature female spikes brown to blackish brown, to 1⅜ in. (35 mm) in diameter. Zone 3.

'Variegata'. Leaves strikingly cream-white striped. Much less vigorous and dramatically less cold hardy than the green-leafed typical form. Superb for container display.

Typha minima
Miniature cat-tail, miniature reedmace

Native to Eurasia. Flowering stems to 32 in. (80 cm) tall. Male and female segments of the inflorescence mostly continuous but sometimes separated by a sterile section. Mature female spikes brown, very shortly cylindrical to nearly round, to 2 in. (5 cm) long and often 1¼ in. (32 mm) in diameter. A superb choice for smaller pools, ponds, and containers. Zone 5.

UNCINIA
Hook sedge (Sedge family)

Comprised of approximately 50 tufted or rhizomatous perennial species closely related to *Carex*, occurring mostly in the Southern Hemisphere, concentrated in Australasia but extending to New Guinea and South and Central America. The ornamental species are low-growing New Zealand natives, all quite similar, prized for their red to red-brown foliage that is evergreen in mild climates. Growing in cool, moist habitats, they thrive when transplanted to places like England and the Pacific Northwest but suffer in the excessive heat common to summers over much of North America. Foliage color varies between seedlings of the same species and is often brighter during the winter months. Flowers are generally insignificant. Propagate by seed or division. Most require

Uncinia rubra in March in a Pennsylvania greenhouse.

well-drained soils and regular moisture and grow best when their roots are kept cool. Grow in full sun in cool climates, in partial shade in warmer zones.

Uncinia egmontiana
Orange hook sedge
Native to New Zealand. Leaves green with orange tints to bright orange, tufted, to 16 in. (40 cm) tall. Zone 8.

Uncinia rubra
Red hook sedge
Native to New Zealand's North and South Islands, mostly in mountainous regions at elevations of 1400 to 4500 ft. (500–1400 m), and nearly to sea level on Stewart Island. Leaves narrow, dark red to bronze-green, tufted, to 14 in. (35 cm) tall. Zone 8.

Vetiveria zizanoides in mid-August in Pennsylvania.

Uncinia uncinata
Hook sedge
Native to New Zealand. Leaves dark bronze-green to brown, tufted, to 18 in. (45 cm) tall. Zone 8.

VETIVERIA
Vetiver (Grass family)
Comprised of 10 perennial species native to flood plains and streambanks in Old World tropics. The following species has been used in medicines and perfumes since prehistoric times and is occasionally grown for ornament.

Vetiveria zizanoides
Vetiver, khus khus, khas khas
Native to the East Indies and escaped from cultivation in the American tropics and the southern United States. An erect, warm-season grower, to 8 ft. (2.4 m) in bloom, the inflorescences narrow panicles produced in late summer in warm climates. Leaves light green, narrow, and erect but characteristically bent backward near their tips. Cultivated for centuries for the aromatic oils concentrated in its rhizomes. Planting for screening effect in warm climates has led to its escape from cultivation; however, khas khas makes a striking container specimen treated as an annual or tender perennial in cold climates, and plants grown in pots rarely flower. The foliage becomes tinted an attractive bronze-purple in autumn. Propagate by division. Zone 9.

ZIZANIA
Wild rice, water rice (Grass family)
Comprised of three species native to marshes and shallow water in North America and eastern Asia. The following two make bold additions to aquatic gardens.

Zizania aquatica
Annual wild rice, Canada wild rice
Native to freshwater and brackish marshes, borders of streams and ponds from Maine to Michigan and Illinois south to Florida and Louisiana.

Zizania aquatica in late October in Pennsylvania.

Mostly annual in the northern United States, occasionally perennial in the southern states. Once the source of edible wild rice, now an expensive delicacy due to labor costs of harvesting. Seeds edible. Flowers in graceful airy panicles to 9 ft. (2.7 m), from midsummer to fall. The lower spikelets are male and have conspicuous yellow pollen sacs. The upper spikelets are female. A stately addition to water gardens, also suited to naturalizing in wet areas. Important as food and shelter for waterfowl, and sometimes planted for these purposes in refuges and game preserves. For use in formal water gardens, start seedlings each year and plant in place in spring. The inflorescences are superb in large cut or dried flower arrangements. Zone 4.

Zizania latifolia in late September in Pennsylvania.

Zizania latifolia
Asian wild rice, Manchurian wild rice

Native to ponds and riverbanks in Indochina, China, Korea, eastern Siberia, and Japan, south through the Ryukyus and Taiwan. The Asian counterpart to North American native *Z. aquatica*, but fully perennial and not as tall. Mostly clump-forming, spreading slowly by rhizomes. Upright to 8 ft. (2.4 m) in flower. Leaves vertical, to 1¼ in. (32 mm) wide, green in summer, turning yellow in fall. Flowers in relatively dense, upright panicles, from mid-August into October. The lower spikelets in each inflorescence are male, the upper female. Prefers shallow water, is useful in shallow ponds, pools, or large containers. Propagate by seed or by division in spring. Zone 7.

USDA HARDINESS ZONE MAP

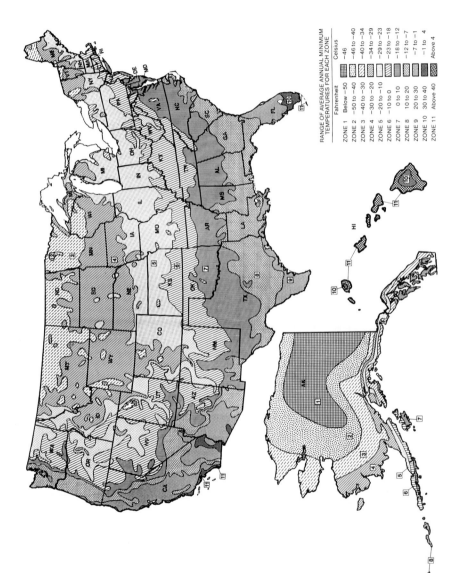

RANGE OF AVERAGE ANNUAL MINIMUM
TEMPERATURES FOR EACH ZONE

	Fahrenheit	Celsius
ZONE 1	Below −50	−46
ZONE 2	−50 to −40	−46 to −40
ZONE 3	−40 to −30	−40 to −34
ZONE 4	−30 to −20	−34 to −29
ZONE 5	−20 to −10	−29 to −23
ZONE 6	−10 to 0	−23 to −18
ZONE 7	0 to 10	−18 to −12
ZONE 8	10 to 20	−12 to −7
ZONE 9	20 to 30	−7 to −1
ZONE 10	30 to 40	−1 to 4
ZONE 11	Above 40	Above 4

EUROPEAN HARDINESS ZONE MAP

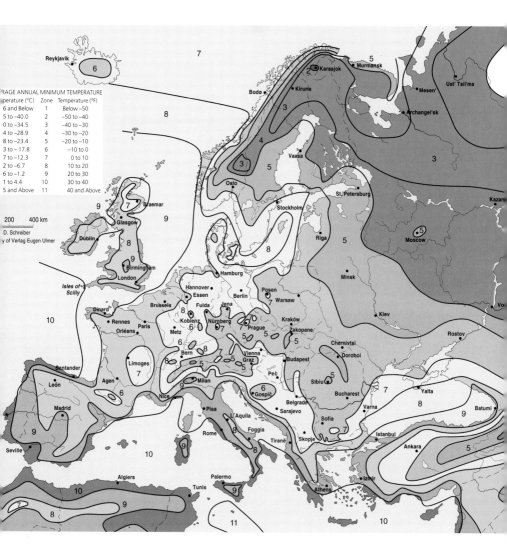

RAGE ANNUAL MINIMUM TEMPERATURE		
perature (°C)	Zone	Temperature (°F)
6 and Below	1	Below –50
5 to –40.0	2	–50 to –40
0 to –34.5	3	–40 to –30
4 to –28.9	4	–30 to –20
8 to –23.4	5	–20 to –10
3 to – 17.8	6	–10 to 0
7 to –12.3	7	0 to 10
2 to –6.7	8	10 to 20
6 to –1.2	9	20 to 30
1 to 4.4	10	30 to 40
5 and Above	11	40 and Above

200   400 km

D. Schreiber
y of Verlag Eugen Ulmer

NURSERY SOURCES

This is a partial list, limited to nurseries in the United States and the United Kingdom that have a specialty in ornamental grasses or bamboos, or that offer grasses that are generally hard to find. Catalogs or lists are available from most. No endorsement is intended, nor is criticism implied of sources not mentioned.

American Ornamental Perennials
29977 SE Weitz Lane
Eagle Creek, Oregon 97022
(503) 637-3095
http://www.gramineae.com

André Viette Farm & Nursery
P.O. Box 1109
Fishersville, Virginia 22939
(800) 575-5538
http://www.viette.com

Apple Court
Hordle Lane, Hordle
Lymington, Hampshire SO41 0HU
United Kingdom
44 (01590) 642130
http://www.applecourt.com

Bald Eagle Nursery
18510 Sand Road
Fulton, Illinois 61252
(815) 589-4121

Bernardo Beach Native Plant Farm
1 Sanchez Road
Veguita, New Mexico 87062
(505) 345-6248

Beth Chatto Gardens Ltd.
Elmstead Market
Colchester, Essex CO7 7DB
United Kingdom
44 (01206) 822007
http://www.bethchatto.co.uk

Blooms of Bressingham
Bressingham, Diss
Norfolk IP22 2AB
United Kingdom
44 (01379) 687386
http://www.bloomsofbressingham.co.uk

Bluebird Nursery
P.O. Box 460
Clarkson, Nebraska 68629
(800) 356-9164
http://www.bluebirdnursery.com

Carroll Gardens
444 East Main Street
P.O. Box 310
Westminster, Maryland 21157
(800) 638-6334
http://www.carrollgardens.com

Comstock Seed
917 Highway 88
Gardnerville, Nevada 89460
(775) 746-3681
http://www.comstockseed.com

Crystal Palace Perennials
P.O. Box 154
St. John, Indiana 46373
(219) 374-9419
http://www.crystalpalaceperennials.com

Digging Dog Nursery
P.O. Box 471
Albion, California 95410
(707) 937-1130
http://www.diggingdog.com

Garden Treasure Nursery
159 Three Mile Harbor Road
East Hampton, New York 11937
(516) 329-3125

Glasshouse Works
Church Street
P.O. Box 97
Stewart, Ohio 45778
(740) 662-2142
http://www.glasshouseworks.com

Granite Seed
1697 West 2100 North
Lehi, Utah 84043
(801) 768-4422
http://www.graniteseed.com

Greenlee Nursery
241 E Franklin Avenue
Pomona, California 91766
(909) 629-9045

Hedgerow Farms
21740 County Road 88
Winters, California 95694
(530) 662-4570
http://www.hedgerowfarms.com

Heronswood Nursery
7530 NE 288th Street
Kingston, Washington 98346
(360) 297-4172
http://www.heronswood.com

Hoffman Nursery
5520 Bahama Road
Rougemont, North Carolina 27572
(800) 203-8590
http://www.hoffmannursery.com

Jelitto Perennial Seeds
125 Chenoweth Lane, Suite 301
Louisville, Kentucky 40207
(502) 895-0807
https://www.jelitto.com

Kurt Bluemel, Inc.
2740 Greene Lane
Baldwin, Maryland 21013
(800) 498-1560
http://www.kurtbluemel.com

Larner Seeds
P.O. Box 407
Bolinas, California 94924
(415) 868-9407
http://www.larnerseeds.com

Limerock Ornamental Grasses
70 Sawmill Road
Port Matilda, Pennsylvania 16870
(814) 692-2272
http://www.limerockgrasses.com

Maryland Aquatic Nurseries
3427 North Furnace Road
Jarrettsville, Maryland 21084
(410) 557-7615
http://www.marylandaquatic.com

Milaeger's Gardens
4838 Douglas Avenue
Racine, Wisconsin 53402
(800) 669-9956

The Natural Garden, Inc.
38W443 Highway 64
St. Charles, Illinois 60175
(630) 584-0150
http://www.thenaturalgardeninc.com

New England Bamboo Company
5 Granite Street
Rockport, Massachusetts 01960
(978) 546-3581
http://www.newengbamboo.com

Niche Gardens
1111 Dawson Road
Chapel Hill, North Carolina 27516
(919) 967-0078
http://www.nichegdn.com

North American Prairies Company
11754 Jarvis Avenue
Annandale, Minnesota 56379
(320) 274-5316
http://www.northamericanprairies.com

Plant Delights Nursery
9241 Sauls Road
Raleigh, North Carolina 27603
(919) 772-4794
http://www.plantdelights.com

Plants of the Southwest
3095 Agua Fria Road
Santa Fe, New Mexico 87507
(505) 438-8888
http://www.plantsofthesouthwest.com

Prairie Moon Nursery
Route 3, Box 1633
Winona, Minnesota 55987
(507) 452-1362
http://www.prairiemoon.com

Prairie Nursery
P.O. Box 306
Westfield, Wisconsin 53964
(800) 476-9453
http://www.prairienursery.com

Prairie Ridge Nursery
9738 Overland Road
Mt. Horeb, Wisconsin 53572
(608) 437-5245
http://www.prairieridgenursery.com

Prairie Seed Source
P.O. Box 83
North Lake, Wisconsin 53064
http://www.ameritech.net/users/rasillon/Seed.html

Native Seeds/SEARCH
526 N 4th Avenue
Tucson, Arizona 85705
(520) 622-5561
http://www.nativeseeds.org

Stock Seed Farms
28008 Mill Road
Murdock, Nebraska 68407
(800) 759-1520
http://www.stockseed.com

Sunlight Gardens
174 Golden Lane
Andersonville, Tennessee 37705
(800) 272-7396
http://www.sunlightgardens.com

Theodore Payne Foundation
10459 Tuxford Street
Sun Valley, California 91352
(818) 768-1802
http://www.theodorepayne.org

Tornello Nursery (bamboo)
P.O. Box 789
Ruskin, Florida 33575
(813) 645-5445
http://www.tornellobamboo.com

Tradewinds Bamboo Nursery
28446 Hunter Creek Loop
Gold Beach, Oregon 97444
(541) 247-0835
http://www.bamboodirect.com

Tree of Life Nursery
33201 Ortega Highway
San Juan Capistrano, California 92693
(949) 728-0685
http://www.treeoflifenursery.com

Wayside Gardens
1 Garden Lane
Hodges, South Carolina 29695
(800) 213-0379
http://www.waysidegardens.com

Weiss Brothers Perennial Nursery
11690 Colfax Highway
Grass Valley, California 95945
(530) 272-7657

White Flower Farm
P.O. Box 50, Route 63
Litchfield, Connecticut 06759
(800) 503-9624
http://www.shepherdseeds.com

Wild Earth Native Plant Nursery
22 Conover Street
Freehold, New Jersey 07728
(732) 308-9777

Wild Seed, Inc.
P.O. Box 27751
Tempe, Arizona 85042
(602) 276-3536

Yucca Do Nursery
P.O. Box 907
Hempstead, Texas 77445
(979) 826-4580
http://www.yuccado.com

GLOSSARY

annual a plant that completes its entire life cycle (from seed to seed) in one year

anther the pollen-producing part of the male flower organ, located at the tip of the slender stalk (called the filament)

awn a slender bristlelike or needlelike appendage extending from a bract; awns may be short and barely conspicuous or they may be many inches long, contributing significantly to the beauty and translucency of grass flowers

blade the flat, expanded portion of the leaf above the sheath; the blade may be reduced or modified in various ways, or be absent altogether

bract a general term for any structure that represents a modified leaf; most commonly used to refer to reduced, leaflike structures associated with inflorescences

calcareous containing much higher than average amounts of calcium or lime

crown the base of the plant

culm the aboveground stem of a grass plant; culms are usually upright but may be horizontal

deciduous a plant that sheds or otherwise loses all its leaves annually, or at certain periods, as opposed to an evergreen plant

dioecious a species with male and female flowers on separate plants

ecotype a group of organisms within a species that are the result of genetic adaptation to conditions in a particular habitat

endemic native and restricted to or occurring only in a particular place; sometimes used in a broader sense to mean native, not introduced or naturalized

evergreen remaining green or living throughout the year

floret in grasses, the collective term for an individual flower plus the enclosing inner and outer bracts

forb a broad-leafed flowering plant, as opposed to the grasses, sedges, and rushes

genotype a group of organisms having the same genetic constitution

grain the single-seeded fruit of true grasses; technically called a caryopsis

inflorescence the flowering portion(s) of a plant, complete with any associated bracts

monoculture a population or planting consisting of only one type of plant

monoecious a species with bisexual florets on each plant

panicle an inflorescence having spikelets at the ends of stalks that branch from the main axis

perennial a plant that lives for more than two years

raceme an inflorescence having individual spikelets attached by short stalks to the unbranched main axis

rhizomatous spreading by rhizomes

rhizome an underground horizontal stem

sheath the lower part of the leaf, originating at a node, which clasps or encircles the stem; in true grasses the sheath usually has overlapping margins; in sedges the sheath is usually fused around the stem

spikelet in grasses, a small spike, consisting of one or more florets attached to a small central axis, together with the basal bracts

sport an individual showing marked variation from the normal type

stigma the pollen-receiving structure; the stigma may be located directly at the top of the ovary or may be separated from the ovary by a short stalk (called the style)

stolon an aboveground horizontal stem

stoloniferous spreading by stolons

terminal located at the tip or top end

tussock a thick tuft

umbel a type of inflorescence in which all flowering branches arise from a central point

FURTHER READING

Brown, Lauren. 1979. *Grasses: An Identification Guide*. Boston: Houghton Mifflin.

Darke, Rick. 1993. *Ornamental Grasses at Longwood Gardens*. Kennett Square, Pennsylvania: Longwood Gardens.

Darke, Rick. 1999. *The Color Encyclopedia of Ornamental Grasses: Sedges, Restios, Cattails, and Selected Bamboos*. Portland, Oregon: Timber Press.

Darke, R., and M. Griffiths, eds. 1994. *Manual of Grasses*. London: Macmillan.

Gleason, Henry A., and Arthur Cronquist. 1991. *Manual of the Vascular Plants of Northeastern United States and Adjacent Canada*. 2nd ed. Bronx: New York Botanical Garden.

Hitchcock, A. S. 1950. *Manual of the Grasses of the United States*. Miscellaneous Publication No. 200, 2nd ed. Rev. by Agnes Chase. Washington, D.C.: U.S. Department of Agriculture.

Holmgren, Noel H. 1998. *Illustrated Companion to Gleason and Cronquist's Manual: Illustrations of the Vascular Plants of Northeastern United States and Adjacent Canada*. Bronx: New York Botanical Garden.

U.S. Department of Agriculture, Natural Resources Conservation Services. 2003. The PLANTS database. Baton Rouge, Louisiana: National Plant Data Center. Available via *http://plants.usda.gov*

INDEX